CW01025098

I THINK OF YOU

Darling Laura,
These come with much
love from your cousin
Bettina and Peter

I THINK OF YOU

& Other Poems

ALEXANDER McCALL SMITH

with illustrations by
IAIN McINTOSH

Merry Christmas
2024

Polygon

First published in hardback in Great Britain in 2023
by Polygon, an imprint of Birlinn Ltd.

Birlinn Ltd
West Newington House
10 Newington Road
Edinburgh EH9 1QS

9 8 7 6 5 4 3 2 1

www.polygonbooks.co.uk

ISBN 978 1 84697 645 2
EBOOK ISBN 978 1 78885 621 8

British Library Cataloguing-in-Publication Data
A catalogue record for this book is available on
request from the British Library.

Typeset in Verdigris MVB by The Foundry, Edinburgh
Printed and bound in Great Britain by Clays Ltd, Elcograf S.p.A.

This book is for Tom Cunningham, composer and friend

CONTENTS

I Think of You

Other Poems

Love, and the human yearning for love, is at the heart of our journey through life. Love is what most people want to find in their lives. When we are very young, we just want a friend. Later, we want a soul-mate. If we are lucky, we find both.

Love, to those who experience it, tends to be a fairly simple thing, a matter of uncomplicated delight. To those who think about it, though, and attempt to understand it, love may be a much more complex matter.

Love has many forms. A common discourtesy is to deny the legitimacy of love that does not conform to a particular set of expectations.

Love preoccupies a great many of us, and it certainly inspires song. 'Scarborough Fair' and *Aida* are at opposite poles of the musical scale and complexity, but are both about the same thing. Love may be expressed by unaccompanied voice, or to the accompaniment of a simple guitar, but it also responds to a large chorus and full orchestration.

'Scarborough Fair' is a song that has origins deep in the folk tradition. When it came to be committed to paper, the accepted version of the lyrics includes the well-known line: 'And tell her to make me a cambric shirt' – a line much misremembered by subsequent singers of this gentle and haunting love song. Some people think it is a *candlewick* shirt that is wanted, not realising, perhaps, that a candlewick shirt would be extremely heavy, candlewick being a suitable material for bedspreads, after all. Others think they hear *camembert shirt*, which would be more uncomfortable. But why a cambric shirt? Why savoury sage, rosemary and thyme?

SCARBOROUGH FAIR

A cambric shirt is here a token
Of feelings felt although unspoken;
It has no language, yet the dove
Still sings a song of undying love;
Both rosemary and its cousin, sage,
Can sorrows in the heart assuage.

Opera, with its capacity for emotional intensity, is an ideal vehicle for the telling of a love story. A love affair on the operatic stage is rarely uncomplicated by rivalry, social barriers, or simple misunderstandings. Sometimes these misunderstandings are simply silly, as in *Così fan tutte*; sometimes they are more profound and feed a growing sense of tragic inevitability, as in *Aida*, which has the claustrophobic ending to end all claustrophobic endings – the entombing together of the star-crossed lovers. Happy endings are more common, and indeed expected, in stage musicals: the von Trapp family crosses the border into Switzerland – had they found themselves in an opera, instead of a musical, they might not have made it.

AIDA

Verdi's point is unobscured
By all the pomp and pyramids:
Love's not simple for these two,
A woman taken from her home,
And a man who's loyal to his cause.

Between pragmatism and the heart,
A stark choice lies: librettists
Make of it a poignant theme;
Enough to fill the opera house,
Night on night, indefinitely.

And the end we never doubt;
Yet even as the orchestra
Begins to think of the last train home,
We weep at these arias
And ask to hear them sung again.

It is true we can live without love – W. H. Auden famously said that, 'Thousands have lived without love, not one without water.' That may be true, but living without love is a hard fate for anyone to bear.

Love is persistent. It survives disappointment and rejection. People may love one another against all the odds, against all the advice of their friends. Love may be a personal disaster as often as it is a glorious triumph. The psalm says 'Many waters cannot quench love.' It goes on to say that it cannot be washed away. Love is ultimately more important than worldly success. Fame and wealth are small things compared with the bedrock security provided by enduring love.

THREE SCOTTISH LOVE POEMS

These three Scottish love poems are based on short stories of no more than a few lines. A story of that length can sometimes describe a whole world, or, as here, a whole love affair.

I knew a young man who had a simple card on which the word *sailor* was printed under his name. There is something to be said for such a simple description of who one is and what one does in this life. A prolix biographical note sometimes tells us more than its author imagines. It suggests self-importance; it reveals a subconscious anxiety that others may have done better; it shows an ego with ambitions for aggrandisement. To describe oneself as a sailor, or a baker, or a carpenter, should be enough. Inscriptions on gravestones should be simple, too, and not make too many claims as to the dignity and good works of the one remembered. In a churchyard in Heysham, in England, there is a stone that reads: *Poet, Philosopher, Failure.* Assuming that he suggested, or at least approved of this epitaph, the subject of that description must have been good and genial company.

A young woman fell in love with a sailor who came from a small town on the Firth of Clyde. He earned his living crewing for yachts being sailed across the Atlantic to Antigua and other places in the Caribbean. He was twenty; she was nineteen. He gave her a card that he had printed. He presented it to her shyly, as one might offer a love token when unsure of its reception. She went off to university and she never saw him again. Yet she thought of him, often.

I. SAILOR

I had a love who went out upon the ocean,
I think of him, with salt upon his skin,
And his few possessions in his cabin
That was almost too small for him
To lie down in and think of me, he said.

He had a little card on which he had printed
His name, and then the single word, *Sailor*,
And I have this now, a tiny poem, a sprig of love,
Upon my shelf, and keep it safe,
And think of him, and the ocean,
And the winds he said would blow to bring him home.

The next story and accompanying poem are about that most poignant of themes – unreciprocated love. Most of us know somebody who has been in love at some time or another with the wrong person – with one who does not return the affection that is felt for him or her. Friends may see this, and may try to persuade the loving one to see the futility of being in love with somebody who is not going to return his love. But sense and reason may not come into it, when one is dealing with matters of the heart. A whole different set of rules may apply there.

Unreciprocated love may seem bleak, but it may nonetheless be something from which a great moral lesson is learned. W. H. Auden proposes just such a lesson in his short poem, 'The More Loving One'. This is a poem that, although only a few lines in length, nonetheless contains what could be a complete philosophy of how to treat others. 'If equal affection cannot be,' Auden says, 'let the more loving one be me.' Extrapolated from the private to the public, that means that even if the world does not love us in the way in which we would like it to, we must nonetheless continue to show love for the world.

'Your House in the Rain' is set in the Scottish Borders. When I wrote it, I had in mind a landscape of rolling hills, swathed in the gentle rain to which Scotland is susceptible. Scottish hills and glens are not infrequently viewed through a veil of light rain moving over the land, so that at one moment the land is obscured, white, and then the next revealed again, dark green, brown, at times purple.

A woman lived in a house in a Borders glen. A man fell in love with her and came to visit her on the occasional Saturday afternoon. She knew what he felt about her, but she had always been in love with somebody else, and wanted to wait for this other man, who worked abroad and rarely returned to Scotland. One afternoon the man who loved her came to see her, and it rained.

II. YOUR HOUSE IN THE RAIN

When I went walking in your glen,
It rained, as it so often feels it must,
In that, and other glens; Scotland
Is a matter of rain, and the concomitants of rain:
Waterfalls, and burns in spate, and washed skies,
The things that make our country half-land, half-water.
   And although I was alone, I thought of you
In your south-facing room, where you like to be,
And I turned and ran back through the rain,
Over the crenellations of mud, stumbling
At the dry-stane dyke, whispering your name
As I passed the hummocks – where a long time ago
Warring factions discovered that peace
Would, on the whole, have been preferable –
To your house, which is always there,
Under the rain, and confirms in its solidity
That you are still there and you still
Do not love me, no matter how I try,
No matter how hard the rain weeps its tears of love.

So many of the important decisions of our life are taken without our being aware of their full significance. The things that happen in our life are not pre-destined, and could easily have been quite different if a single, apparently unimportant event had not occurred or had occurred a few moments earlier or later. Philosophers who have considered this refer to the *moral luck* that may shape our lives. Luck is moral when it affects the decisions that one makes, which may, of course, have important moral implications. Bad moral luck: falling, by chance, into bad company and ending up acting in an anti-social manner. Good moral luck: being born to loving parents who bring you up with a sound sense of right and wrong. This is reflected in the expression, *There but for the grace of God go I.*

In the story that follows, had the cyclist not been knocked over, her whole life would have been different. That means that had she set off on her journey a single minute later, none of what happened to her would have happened.

A woman cyclist was hit by a car when riding on a back road in Glasgow. Another driver stopped and sat with her while they waited for the ambulance. She asked for his telephone number, so that she could thank him later on. They met again, and three months later they went off to live together in Ayrshire, in a former miner's cottage. He had a job on a dairy farm. She taught children of nursery-school age.

III. THE DAIRYMAN & THE TEACHER

When the day began, I made the strong coffee
That he liked to have at that early hour
Before the mists cleared, to reveal fields
Still showing their white latticework of rime.

When the sun went down, he made for me
The infusion that I liked to drink, of favoured herbs,
With my cold feet almost in the fire,
And the easy crossword half completed,
He would clatter about the kitchen,
And then disappear into a steaming bath.

That is how we lived, fortunate in our tiny habits,
Far from the great disputes and ambitions of this world;
I would wish such peace and simple happiness
For everyone, but particularly for those
Who live their lives with the various sorts of fear.

At night, we leave the curtain open;
We like to see the moon, our quiet night-light,
We like to hear the wind that comes
From somewhere far away, beyond our shores,
But kisses Scotland goodnight at each day's end.

THE HEART'S ENGAGEMENTS

I.

For every lover who might be convinced
His happiness was always meant to be,
A discovery awaits; the heart's engagements,
For all their script of perfect sunsets,
Are arbitrary and unplanned, except
In the most grimly fatalistic
Of philosophies – those systems
That leave us not much of a say
In what becomes of us, or of others.
Love is an accident, and like
Just about every accident, it occurs
When you are doing something else,
Collecting the shopping, walking to work,
Or innocently reading the newspaper.
Love is never timely; love never arrives
According to the timetable, like an Italian
Railway train under autocratic government.

II.

Nor is love a matter of desert:
The undeserving and the selfish
May be loved by the kind and considerate;
Those of unmerchantable quality,
By any standards, may still attract
The attention of the discerning
And the gifted; bad matches

May turn out well after all,
As when the bully or the brute
Discovers kindness and a perfect angel
Who softens a hardened heart,
And makes of him a kindly lover;
That happens, sometimes, in books.

III.

Love has never been a matter of fairness,
Aphrodite's reputation, such as it is,
Was never based on having an eye
For what is right and choosing accordingly:
Her young and naked bowman
Has an aim that can be haphazard,
Even if his misplaced darts
Are occasionally welcome where they land;
Love is governed by roulette odds:
Depends on a profile, or a look,
Having nothing to do, in so many cases,
With temperament or ability
To empathise – that is everything to do
With friendship, which is a field
Into which Eros is not meant to wander.
Friendship ripens into love but is not
The sort of love that makes us ache,
Behave unreasonably, or mope
Around the house for days on end;
Friendship makes us do none of that.

IV.

What we hope for in love, at least
When we have had enough experience
To know the way that it works,
Is acceptance – of our faults,
Our limitations, our failure to be
All that others would like us to be;
Love understands, rather than judges,
Reassures the least of us; convinces us
That we are not alone; allows the use
Of the first-person plural
When the single form is just too lonely:
We and *us* have always been more natural
To a social species than *I* and *me*.

V.

Finding love is never easy,
Except for those who, blessed
With beauty, make it seem
Effortless and expected;
We all know one who has only to smile
And hearts are broken;
Oddly, love eludes some like them,
Love's tributes lie at their feet,
But may seem empty, undeserved;
Garlands wilting and ignored
Because they fell too easily, perhaps.

VI

Girls may fall in love with one another,
And the same is true of boys,
Love is indifferent to the conventions
Of chromosomes; Jonathan and his David
Were touching in their devotion,
In their hills and high places,
And today, after long years
Of disapproval and unkindness
We see that it hardly matters:
Boy meets boy and girl meets girl
Is nothing to be embarrassed about:
All love is the same delight
In another; keeping a name
Upon lips gives us pleasure
Whatever that name may be.

VII

Of all the themes by which
A writer lives, love unrequited
Is one of the greatest; there is
Something noble about those
Who nurture a passion for another
Who cannot or who will not
Reciprocate their love:
One of the great subjects of literature
Is nevertheless, for those involved,
A sad business of tissues
Soaked with tears, of bleakness,

Of long waiting for a sign that never comes:
Pity the unrequited love that never is.

VIII

We may lose the one we love
In so many and such different ways,
All of them, it seems to us,
At the time of loss at least,
Uniquely, personally cruel, and undeserved;
Affection may wane, just as we go off
A cardigan we used to like
Or a painting we've grown out of;
Another may catch our lover's eye
With offers we can never match –
Novelty, for one; or oceans
May intervene between us:
It is hard for one in Anchorage
To love another in Adelaide,
Even with electronic assistance;
Or the one we love may simply go away;
That happens too, and may be irreversible.
And yet love shares with Persephone,
With Diana, and all the rest,
A certain immortality; love persists
In memory, and is always there,
Ready to remind us of what it was we had,
A quiet, insistent whisper in the heart.

A FEW COMMENTS ON THESE:

I. Of course love is unscheduled. Nobody says: 'At two o'clock next Wednesday afternoon, I shall fall in love.' We might also remind ourselves that conception might take place well after the necessary event. 'He was conceived while his mother stood in front of the fruit counter in the local supermarket.' That is quite possible, without the occurrence of any public spectacle: conception may take place within minutes or up to five days after the initial act. This is not a romantic thought – but many scientific facts are distinctly unromantic.

The mention of the Italian railways is a reference to the observation made in the 1930s that Mussolini, in spite of everything else that might be held against him, made the trains run on time. Such observations were made ironically – one hopes.

II. Undeserving louts are often loved by loyal and generous women. We all know of such cases and ask, 'What does she see in him?' Sometimes one suspects that she thinks she can reform him. That seldom happens.

III. There is often no justice in love. Love may depend on a dimple. Blondes have more fun. Having a dimple or being blonde is not anything for which anybody can take moral credit. It's very unfair.

IV. Love is indeed forgiving. And as for the need for others, for company rather than singularity, that is universal. Sometimes, indeed, we pluralise the second person singular in order to make the other feel less isolated. In her novel *The Conservationist*, a novel of grave beauty, Nadine Gordimer describes a farmer addressing a single neighbour as 'you people' out of the polite assumption that everybody must have somebody. I remember being surprised, when I lived for a short time in Dallas, by the expression 'you-all' (y'all). This is used when talking to one person – another instance,

I imagine, of what we might call the complimentary plural. In Scotland, one person may be addressed as *youse* – perhaps for the same reason. More than one person becomes *youses*.

V. The beautiful are easy to love. They may take it as their due and not think much about it. How tiresome it must be to have everybody swooning at one's feet. The rest of us don't want *that*. No, not at all.

VI. It doesn't matter whom one chooses to love. Giving people the right to make that choice was one of the great moral steps forward of the second half of the twentieth century. Unfortunately, there are places in the world where that step has not been taken and people still suffer sexual oppression.

VII. Unrequited love is important for poets and novelists. If love is too easy, then there is not much to write about. Opera thrives on love's difficulties too. *Madama Butterfly* would be much shorter without the hurdles faced by the lovers. Similarly, *La bohème* would not be the moving opera it is if antibiotics had been available to Mimi.

VIII. Loving often involves loss – indeed, loss is the inevitable final stage of any love affair. Yet, in spite of the loss that it entails, love persists – and insists.

Valentine's Day is, of course, still widely celebrated. This is a Valentine's Day poem. Such poems need no explanation: they are simple statements of the feeling that one person has for another. Sometimes that feeling is an ache. Sometimes it is a flutter of the heart. Sometimes it starts with self-reproach, as in this poem, and then moves on to acceptance. Love requires no apology, no looking over the shoulder, no expression of regret. It simply is.

THE APPLE IS WRONGLY AWARDED

Young Paris, rescued by shepherds
From a stern father's filicidal measures,
Prevailed upon to award an apple,
Tossed in envy, listened, unwisely,
To the sales pitch of three
Contending for the title of fairest;

   Never judge a beauty competition,
Is advice any Dutch uncle may offer
A young man; heedless, Paris
Succumbed to Aphrodite's promise
Of Helen's attentions, while Athena
Looked sadly on; she knew only too well
How a judgement like that would end;
Nothing new happens in myth,
Which is the whole point,
Our psychic dramas being an old story;

   Had Paris chosen Athena, with her wit,
Her command of the arts and of science,
He, and the rest of us, would have been
Much happier in the long run;
Beauty is skin deep; physical attraction
Starts Trojan Wars; choose the one you love
On the basis of qualities you cannot see –
Loyalty, humour, tenderness,
All deserving of an apple, at the very least,
Things that never lose their ability
To create happiness, grow with the years,
Rather than fade and fail, as human beauty will;
Paris will find that out, as finally do we all.

Finally, a fitting end to this section. This could be about a lover or a friend, or anybody, I suppose, whom one likes and whom one is prepared to admit, quite frequently, and fondly, to one's thoughts.

I THINK OF YOU

I think of you, as sometimes we think
Of those who, fortunately,
Do not diminish with time,
Whose clarity is undimmed,
Who never merge with the crowd
In the confusion of the daily play
In which we all are actors.

I think of you at odd moments
When my thoughts should be elsewhere,
When some task makes technical demands
And concentration is required;
I think of you in spite of that.

I think of you on Scottish moors
Where the hills recede into indeterminate blue
And mountains with fond local names
Stand guard over secrets long forgotten,
And the sky changes in an instant,
Bringing sun, or rain; I think of you then.

I think of you when I hear the news
Of things happening elsewhere,
And the voice of the announcer is grave
Because somewhere there is suffering
As the world pursues its accustomed cruelties;
I think of you, and of how your kindness
Is the opposite of all that.

Love Letters to Edinburgh

IN THIS CITY
A love letter to Edinburgh

Sometimes, in the fullness of summer,
Scotland may forget its geographical position,
May fail to recall the latitudes
That are its boundaries, that define
Where the Borders start and where
Shetland and its most northerly lighthouse
Meet a sea in which there is no further
Evidence of land, and over which
That lighthouse sends a glimmer,
A pinprick of light in a night
That in winter lasts a very long time.

In such conditions of summer optimism,
Edinburgh, persuading itself of the possibilities
Of an external life, populates its pavements
With crowds and performers and cafés.
While, in democratic profusion, flags
And banners of all kind indiscriminately
Advertise the spirit of festival,
Allude to art and to all the themes
That art embraces; and remind us
That this, after all, is the city of Ramsay,
Of the wigmaker-poet who collected
All those songs and stories of place;
Of Robert Fergusson, who briefly
Caught the rhythm of a language
Before another arrived from Ayrshire
To entertain the well-to-do here

With the poetry of those who had
So very much less than they had,
But who still were generous and unbowed;
While philosophers, dreamers each
Of another way at looking at the world,
Blew away the cobwebs that survive
Only in darkness and in superstition;
All this diminishes, of course, as years intervene,
But descend to the Cowgate,
By those stone steps worn down
By generations of feet, and listen
To the heartbeat of a city
That still wants so keenly to say
Something to the world;
That would still wish, although it's so late,
To make the general statement,
And embrace the human and humane;
It has not departed, that spirit
That lies so light on this city,
Its touch a gentle one, barely felt,
Its voice a whisper, but as persistent
As an echo that determines not to fade.

I wrote the next Edinburgh poem for a charity set up by the philanthropist Jack Stewart-Clark, to help people in Scotland who have been trafficked. The theme is freedom – the setting Edinburgh. The poem was to be a song for a fundraising concert. Then everything stopped as the pandemic took hold, and the song was never performed. The music for the song was written by Tom Cunningham, with whom I have collaborated, as librettist, on numerous song cycles and chamber operas. The metre here is chosen for its suitability for song.

THE SUN ON PRINCES STREET

On Saturday we stopped and gazed
On Princes Street, on Princes Street,
As unexpected came the sun
And kissed the stone of Princes Street,
And up above us, all the flags
Fluttered brave on Princes Street,
In semaphore they made the claim
Of freedom there on Princes Street.

And somewhere, in a place nearby,
A brass band played – you knew the tune,
And mouthed the words on Princes Street;
The message of the song, you said,
Was ae fond kiss, as Burns would say;
While up above us in the sky
The pigeons fluttered, fanning out;
A train passed by, it whistled sharp
On Princes Street, on Princes Street,
The heart can break, you pointed out,
In many ways, in many ways,
And most of them, it seemed to me,
On Princes Street, on Princes Street.

THE IDEA OF METAPHOR IN
NORTH EDINBURGH

One thing, we know, may always be
Something other than the thing
It appears to be; although certainty
Keeps us rooted where we feel secure,
A discovery awaits: reality
Is subjective; every child,
In his small room, scared of the dark,
Understands this patent truth:
A darkened shape is often not
The thing that Mother says it is;
Chairs and cupboards may appear
To be wild beasts, or burglars, too,
Bent on malice, each lurking,
Waiting for the chance to strike;

  A bedside light once switched on
May reduce these shadowed threats
To a shape and size more natural to
An average bedroom inventory,
But in the darkness, terror is real.

Yet even when the day returns
That which now we recognise
May show itself as something else:
Thus, a proverbial darkening cloud
No bigger than a human hand,
May be a double metaphor
Both for smallness and for threat,
Combined for greater potency;

A handshake may turn out to be
A mode of passing on disease
In a time of high anxiety,
Or just a sign of fellowship,
A gesture of shared humanity;
Infection, after all, is human, too,
And so the offering of a hand
Becomes a semiotic recipe
For everything we love and fear.

A game of tennis is not about
Accuracy and forearm strength,
But is more a matter of potency,
And of sex, of course; tennis players
Know that well; one hardly needs
To point to all the work that *love*
Does in Wimbledon, in keeping score;
Wimbledon itself is just a metaphor
For an entire game, a whole afternoon,
And for strawberries, rich and red,
Like flesh, inviting lovers' bites.

Even a bird may be a bird,
Or a metaphor for being free:
Icarus may be a youth
Or a warning; he may even be
An issue for the engineers;
   Above the grave of Orpheus,
Nightingales, we're told, still sing,
Metaphors each for what we feel,
For a meaning underneath the skin.

Kindness, Friendship

&

Making Sense of Things

If there is a single human quality that most of us value above others it is kindness. I had a friend whose family motto was beautifully simple: *Be Kind*. That was all it said. And he lived up to that throughout his rather short life. What more does one need? Kindness requires no explanation or elaboration. Be kind to others – not a difficult proposition. In the words of Mozart's sublime trio in *Così fan tutte*, 'Soave sia il vento' – 'may the breeze that carries you through life be a gentle one'. That is what we might wish for those we encounter on our journey.

Living a good life is not always easy. One thing is certain, though, and that is that following fashion – doing what everybody else around you is doing – is no way to conduct one's life. There is no merit in being a sheep – unless of course, one *is* a sheep.

This poem is about being old-fashioned. Once again, there is no particular merit in that; old things are not necessarily venerable simply because they are old. But in the practices and the attitudes of the past, one may discover things that are worthwhile. This poem is intended to give comfort to those who know that they should not be worried if people consider them out of step with the *Zeitgeist*. Be yourself, even if you appear passé. Don't worry if you seem old-fashioned and out-of-touch – the pendulum has a habit of swinging, and you may find that your old clothes are suddenly the height of fashion. It's all a question of being prepared to wait long enough.

SO YESTERDAY

Among the reproaches by which
We signal disapproval of those we know,
Some are clearly capable
Of only one interpretation:
To say to others, 'You look awful'
Suggests that they do:
Awfulness is hard to view
In a positive light,
Which is an awful state of affairs
But stubbornly the case.

But then there is 'You look
So last year', or, worse still,
'You are . . .' and in the space
You insert a decade,
Usually a long time ago;
As in 'You are so nineteen-sixties',
Which can be met by an injured
And reproachful silence,
But need not be: not if you think
For a moment about the merits
Of the decades we've put behind us.

I am, I admit, so *last year* myself,
I like clothes that don't fit
Too tightly, allow for expansion;
I like soap that smells of soap
And not of Keralan pepper
Or obscure botanicals, that comes

In boxes labelled simply 'Soap';
I like milk from which
Nothing has been extracted,
That can be used to make
All sorts of illegal cheese;
I like telephones connected
To the world by a wire;
I like strangers who say 'good morning'
Even though they have no idea
Whether you deserve a greeting;
I like men who take the risk
Of letting women walk through doors
Ahead of them, rather than racing
To go through first; I like
Children who speak politely;
I like everyone who talks in sentences
That somewhere contain a verb; I like films
In which few people die,
And hardly any of the actors
Swear at one another, or at the world;
I like dogs of recognisable breed
Or simple mongrels, not those
Bearing names bolted together:
Labradoodles and so on; I like
Honest dogs who don't question
Why the ball or stick must be fetched,
And who sit when commanded,
Sometimes for hours; I like
All these unfashionable things,

Although I know you will say
'You're so irredeemably yesterday!'
I like yesterday, in fact,
I liked it then, and I still do;
When I think of tomorrow, I think
Of yesterday, and of how it glowed.

But let us not romanticise the past. The past was full of injustice and suffering (rather like the present, in that respect). Before you say that you would not have minded living in a past epoch, in some golden age of your imagining, remember that dental anaesthesia was invented only relatively recently; that antibiotics were undreamed of, with the result that a mere scratch could result in sepsis and rapid death; and that we didn't live for all that long anyway. The era of human rights and social welfare has a great deal to commend it, even if we sometimes feel that the modern world is too crowded, too noisy, and too stressful. And hot water – that great boon to domestic life, that great promoter of cleanliness and soother of aching limbs; that great facilitator of the smooth shave – has been around for a long time, but it was often in the wrong place at the wrong time. The Romans, though, were good plumbers. We owe them a great debt for mastering the art of transferring heat through a building, of inventing the means by which the daily soak in the tub might be available to the least of us.

HOT WATER

I.

Roman engineers believed it true
That water could be tasked
To help our human enterprise
As all elements can, if asked.

Endowed by its geology
With bisecting mountain ridges,
Italy is a vertebrate
Ripe for aqueducts and bridges.

They built their public works so that
Through gutters and through runnels
Water reached the citizens
Through passages and tunnels.

II.

Heated water made reveille
So much less of an ordeal,
In the cooler parts of an empire
Stretching from lambent sun to ice;

And nobody protested at
The trouble involved, nor the cost:
Hot water was always welcome
Whenever it made its entrance.

For philosophers remind us:
Stoicism is less demanding
In a heated environment
Free from unwanted icy draughts;

And water serves local purpose:
In Iceland, geothermal pools
Have been considered cultural
Rather than hygienic projects;

And even today, as we soak
In an abundance of hot water
We might reflect: without this,
How cold is the alternative;

How uncomfortable is the life
In which hot water has never
Been a possibility, how
Dependent we are on plumbing.

Gratitude – whether it is for the invention of modern plumbing, or simply for the inestimable privilege of just being alive – is worth expressing. We are sometimes slow to say thank you, but the power of those two words is hard to overestimate. Thanking another for something that other has done gives great pleasure to the recipient of the thanks. It makes his or her work seem worthwhile; it imparts a sense of having done something worthwhile: it validates. And it is terribly easy – it requires no rehearsal, no sacrifice, no special words. Just thanks.

Thanking those who operate the public services on which we rely is particularly important. In Edinburgh, it is common for people alighting from buses to thank the driver. In not every city is this done. Yet it is typical of those small courtesies on which our life in society is founded, and is worth doing.

This poem was written in gratitude to those people who run the health service. They are just doing their job, of course, but they tend to do it with kindness and concern for those who are ill, in pain, or just plain frightened. This is institutional kindness – a great good in a troubled and at times threatening world.

LOOKED AFTER

None of us remembers that first meeting –
Tumbling out into a very different world,
Into your receiving hands,
Blinking at the light; we breathed
The strangeness of oxygen,
Saw the unfamiliar walls
Of the delivery room,
And the first ceiling we had ever
Looked at, and wondered what it was.

That was the first thing
You did for us: welcomed us,
Ushered us into infancy
And childhood, and the years beyond.
We never thanked you
But do so now, rather late,
But with all the feeling
Of the long overdue
Expression of gratitude,
The tardy repayment
Of an ancient debt.

Since then, from time to time,
You have picked us up,
Dusted us down, bandaged
The occasional consequence
Of our failure to look
Where we're going

Or to behave quite as we might;
Tolerant, like all good
Members of your profession,
You said nothing, but did
What was necessary.
And sent us on our way,
Patched up and healed.

Now, quite suddenly, we call on you,
And the call is an urgent one.
You are there, of course, it never
Occurred to you that you would be
Anywhere else than at our side.
Hour after hour, day after day,
You are there, the support
Of those hands that first delivered us
Embracing us once again,
With the same love, the quiet
And gentle care; once again
We spell out our debt, our gratitude,
You say, 'It's what we do.'
We nod and say, 'We always knew.'

Near-death experiences are the subject of much discussion. Those who have experienced them are adamant that they have been vouchsafed a vision of an existence beyond death. They describe moving through a tunnel towards light; they describe encounters with other beings. They often feel profoundly changed by what they had experienced before the defibrillator brought them back to life.

Whether or not these experiences are real, or are simply the result of an oxygen-starved brain, is a matter of dispute. But whatever one thinks of near-death experiences, we might pay more attention to what could be called *near-life experiences*. These occur at moments when we suddenly feel the full possibilities of life – moments of mystical insight. We have all had these, in varying degrees of intensity.

THE NEAR-LIFE EXPERIENCE

They speak with certainty once they've woken up,
Tell of a warming light, welcoming and bright,
That lit the way ahead with gentleness,
That beckoned them within with tenderness;
That is what they recall, those images all
That they bring back from the brief oblivion
Of unconsciousness, concomitants of the condition
That those who investigate such things
Call the near-death experience, simply that.

The near-life experience is something rather different,
Happens when you are still unambiguously alive
And certainly not expecting anything unusual,
As when, on a perfectly ordinary morning,
The anniversary of nothing in particular,
You see the sun float up over a line of trees
And briefly the world is golden; birds,
Undistinguished otherwise, begin their song,
Their calls of love and territory,
The orations that accompany their search
For love and for somewhere to live,
Things that we, like they, rather wish
Were generally available, and in greater profusion;

Or when, in conversation with a friend,
You suddenly realise how much you cherish
The other's otherness, your sharing
Of life's path, and reach across a table
To join hands, or touch each other's shoulder

Or forearm, and feel suddenly happy,
When otherwise you never thought you would
Be granted a near-life experience;

Or when, listening to the familiar notes
Of music you have always responded to, and wished
That, things being different, you could play
As beautifully and with such accomplishment
As these allocated musicians effortlessly do;
And yet now, a listener, you understand
Why a particular chord had to be
Precisely where it was, and how the heart
Has responded to a cadence, found in it
Resolution that the world can never give;
All this is annotated on the score:
An experience of the possible, nothing more.

This poem is about saying goodbye. The final verse may be extracted and used to say goodbye to a friend – in whatever circumstances, including a final farewell. As Mma Ramotswe puts it, 'late people are still with us'. Of course they are.

HOW TO SAY GOODBYE

Each year we find ourselves surprised
By the rapidity with which summer
Shrugs off its leaves, leaving the stage
To a windier customer, not inhibited
From showing us his braggadocio;
And so it is with other things that end,
We may look up and see they've gone
Before we had the time to say *Don't go*,
And all that's left is bonfire smoke
And memories of light and warmth.

Few things end without a note
Alerting us to transience;
As children, the world in which we live
Is secure in immortality,
As we are too; there's always time,
Until suddenly we learn there's not;
That is how it works, we're told,
When we protest against the fact.

And so, goodbyes, which might have been
Provisional, are final now;
Inoculation against life's pain
Is unavailable in our ordinary disease;
Loss is natural, which makes our world
So precious; no one, ever, has successfully
Fought a campaign against it, nor would wish
To be the failed Canute of such a cause.

The proper language of farewell
Is spoken quietly, and with regret,
Makes no claims to what it cannot
Possibly deliver – gives no promises;
And yet goodbye, which is a word
Whose meaning we often learn too late,
Still leaves us well provided for:
Your smile is sunshine on the hills,
Your laughter is the chuckle
Of a burn; your kindness is the way
The earth continues to provide
Ripening grain and pendant fruit,
Things you've left behind, have given us.

SEPTEMBER 1, 2022

In homage to W. H. Auden

This particular morning dawns
Like any other in early autumn,
Unremarkable, apart from the date
To which an event a long time ago
Gave especial significance, a haunting
Of a sort our rueful calendars
Have become quite accustomed to;
Where are we now? The question
Frightened children always ask
When, lost in a wood, they fail
To see a way out; the trees
Press in, the trunk of each bears
A label with a specified warning,
And the inventory is a long one:
A war has already begun on fields
That once grew an abundance of wheat
And now grow mines, and the craters
That mines produce; how many lives
Have ended in sudden detonation?
The newspapers have the answers.

We know so much now:
All human knowledge, we are told,
Can be found on a single chip;
Yet nowhere is there an answer,
Or at least nowhere is there
An answer that we'd really care
To pay attention to;
If there were a bar into which

The thirsty might quietly slip,
The talk inside would probably be
Of things quite unconnected
With our own and immediate crisis,
Or the needs of a suffering world –
And understandably so: few
Frequent bars to address their doubts.
    But still there are those
Who valiantly continue to affirm;
They are recognisable, marked
By a feeling for the future
That the rest of us seem to have lost;
We turn to them for a prescription
Now that the other pharmacies
Are closed; we wait for their message
About honesty, its importance,
And the seriousness of purpose
We momentarily lost; we hear
Them say that we must clear the stage
Of the actors whose grease paint
Concealed something we knew
Was wrong for us, for our fragile world;
We learn, at last, the lesson we teach
As a didactic nursery rhyme
To small and selfish children:
Those who have a lot of stuff
Should share with those without enough.

This is a poem that I imagined being written by a fictional character in one of my books, the Captain in *The Captain's Cabin*. Here the Captain remembers a friend who became a doctor and went off to Uganda to work in a hospital there. We lose touch with old friends; seas move between us; and yet we may wish to keep alive the thought of reunion.

The reference to 'that emergency' in the line that precedes the pre-ante-penultimate line – to put it simply – is, of course, the Second World War. People have spoken of great crises in these terms in the past, as if one might somehow tame a conflagration by the use of an innocent term. The lengthy military campaign in Malaysia between 1948 and 1960 was officially called 'the Emergency' because if it had been called a civil war the insurance industry would not have met claims for loss – such claims being refused if they arose in the context of war. Ireland called the Second World War 'the Emergency'.

That can be the language of denial, but it can also be the language of stoicism – as it is, I think, in this case.

SINCE YOU WENT AWAY

Dear friend, since you went away
I've written twice, failed to post the letter,
Fearing you might not find the time
To bother with my thoughts;
    Friendship is something that is hard to paint
In words, in ink, on something so insubstantial
As a piece writing paper; an orchestra,
Complete with chorus, is what friendship deserves,
But very rarely gets; love requires that too,
Although I have never quite understood
The distinction between the two,
Perhaps I shall on that dreadful day
When we say a real goodbye,
And I shall cry buckets, as I know I shall,
In my ordinary conviction that we always
Had something particular to say to one another;
Seas between us move, that island we both knew,
Is green still; Ben Mhor still surveys
The places we walked in that emergency;
The boat I would send for you, if ever I do,
Will be frail, will be delicate;
Wait for it by the shore, do not let it pass.

The idea of sending a boat for a friend is a beguiling one. It suggests an image from Tang poetry in which a credible image might be that of an exiled functionary waiting by the river for the boat that will bring a friend to visit him, in his lonely durance. 'Crying buckets' is what we do when we are truly upset: to say to a friend 'I shall cry buckets at your funeral' is a touching compliment, rather than an unwelcome prediction of an imminent event.

Speech and writing need their signposts. Punctuation does that – and like the rules of the road, should be taken seriously. Language without punctuation is hard to follow and to understand, and language like that can easily be subverted and rendered meaningless. Clarity in language is one of our greatest protections against tyranny. Tyrants actively seek to subvert meaning; despots are only too happy for us to be linguistically confused – that gives them far more scope for lies and distortion. George Orwell alerted us to that. He was remarkably prescient. So, punctuation is really important – it matters, as the title of the following poem suggests.

I. BEFORE THERE WAS PUNCTUATION

Before we stumbled, innocent, on punctuation,
Words frequently followed one another
In a stream, meant something, perhaps,
But were hard to decipher, a bit like a dream,
Had little meaning, or so it would seem.

Before punctuation was revealed to us,
Everything was joined together
In a continuous line, never gave time
For the taking of breath or for reflection,
Rarely disclosing the speaker's true intention.

II. THE DISCOVERY OF THE COMMA

Happy the day they found
That in between thoughts
A small mark, suspended,
Could us give time to breathe,
Could say that, and now this,
Which comes immediately after,
Although it still relates
To what has gone before.

And suddenly, there was the comma,
And the long hike of sentences
Could now be marked
With resting places –
Oases in a featureless desert;
Places of shade and refreshment,
Where tents of parentheses
Might be pitched.

Grammarians, nomads all,
Traded merchantable commas
In street markets and in *souks*;
Lent them to us generously,
Said: 'Don't forget to use them.'

III. THE APOSTROPHE

Unfortunate is the use of this device
Where the rules state clearly
It should be scrupulously avoided;
Regrettable are the ubiquitous signs
That say, NO DOG – *apostrophe* – S ALLOWED.
If dogs fail to understand
And impose themselves regardless,
That is purely because
The apostrophe is wrong,
The point will never be conceded:
Apostrophes should be used
Only where they are really needed.

By night the tireless purists
Police the messages on notice boards,
Rub out the apostrophes
Where none should be,
Risk arrest to stop the rot.
Heroic still, this battle rages,
Unwinnable, it's thought,
And yet they persist:
This rule, they say, really ought
To be defended, this battle fought.

IV. THE SEMI-COLON

This is for use when it is time for a break,
Though not for one in which
We may wish to sit down,
Stretch out, remove our boots,
Possibly nod off until, insistently,
The call for departure sounds again.
This is for use when we need
To look about us, take stock briefly,
Perhaps change direction
By a couple of degrees – no more.

The semi-colon allows the reader
To catch up with the writer;
'Are you still there?' the writer asks,
And the reader replies: 'I am,
And am ready once again
To hear what you have to say;
Please proceed – after your semi-colon';
After the full stop over the comma
Has done its work, and the signal
Has once more turned to green.

V. THE DASH

The dash is easy to deploy,
Requires the briefest movement
Of the punctuating wrist:
One stroke, it promises
An explanation, a resolution.

Why did something happen?
Let the dash reveal
The events that led us to this point.
Who was present, who was there?
Let the dash precede
The list of names.
What will happen now?
Let the dash suggest
We know the answer,
Although we don't;
None of us, I'm afraid to say,
Really knows; the dash, though,
Is full of confidence,
Smooths out the contours
Of uncertainty, and the dark.

VI. THE FULL STOP

Everything has to end,
Even history; nothing
Can go on for ever,
Much as we would like it to.
A full stop endorses
The insight that children grasp:
Enough will always be enough,
The finest sunset, after dusk,
Must fade, the best of parties
Break up as the guests leave;
Everything has an end,
Even the best-constructed sentence
Must have a full stop when it's through;
My dear, I thought love and friendship
Never ended; I was wrong: they do.

And now, on to division. We are not keen on large, vaguely defined wholes; we wish, as a species, to impose order on that which is without particular form – such as the day itself. We want routines, so that we know what to expect; so that we don't have to guess what will happen next. On ships, bells were rung to mark the watches of the day. These watches, still observed in navies, are four-hour segments: first, middle, forenoon, afternoon, followed by two dog-watches. In monasteries, the canonical hours by which the day is divided are: *lauds, prime, terce, sext, none, vespers* and finally *compline*.

We may still feel a need for divisions of the day. The hours proposed here reflect the concerns of our modern existence, starting with *Anxiety (three a.m.)*, and going on to *Dawn (six a.m.)*, *Coffee (nine a.m.)*, *Luncheon (noon)*, *Siesta (three p.m.)*, *Reflection (six p.m.)* and *Cocoa (nine p.m.)*.

ANXIETY

(three a.m.)

Those who wake at this particular hour,
Half-way between midnight and a dawn
That is yet to announce itself convincingly,
Might be forgiven for feeling concerned
Over the things they imagine they see;
Every shadow, innocent enough in daylight,
Is more suggestive now of something
We might not especially care to meet;
Every minute, brief enough in morning,
Takes rather longer in these small hours
To make the journey from present to past,
And is indifferent to our desire for day;
Your metabolism, time whispers,
Cannot be hurried: if the world at three
Seems bleak, that's because it is.

The scholar in his patient cell
Hears the sound of muffled bell,
Knows that learning never could
Remove the terrors of the wood
Amongst whose trees each human heart
Is separate and must live apart.

DAWN

(six a.m.)

Those who understand the nature of birdsong
Appreciate its territoriality, point out
That what may seem a joyful tribute
To some avian god we've yet to meet
Is really something quite different, revealing
That in those small and transient arboreal lives
There are major issues of borders
And access to food – all those things
That make our own lives so difficult –
Yet are rendered so deceptively joyous
In the sharp sweetness of song.
    Perhaps the things we see and hear
Are best not fully understood, but sensed instead;
Most, I imagine, would prefer to believe
That beauty and concord really do exist,
Are not a vague promise, but with us now,
Can be heard and experienced at dawn,
Are regular in their performance,
Generous in their encores, sung
Entirely in sympathetic keys,
And require from us no payment.

COFFEE
(nine a.m.)

In that it divides the morning
Into equal segments of three hours,
In which something, but not too much,
May be achieved; it is welcomed by all.

In that it allows the slow-to-awake
Who are not at their best after breakfast
To appear sharp enough, and capable
Of making sense; it is helpful to most.

In that it brings to the air about it
A smell that everyone likes and savours,
Ranking above other olfactory treats,
Evocative of imagined cafés; it is harmless enough.

In that we can give it up without
Excessive withdrawal symptoms
And go back to it, grateful, without too heavy
A sense of failure; it need not embarrass.

In that it is coffee, and it brings
To all a mild sense of wellbeing;
Kills very few, makes most happier,
Forfends strokes; it is deserving of its hour.

LUNCHEON

(noon)

Underneath a sky that, for the moment at least,
In spite of its record of dampening ambitions
With an inconsiderate vindictive downpour,
Allows the customary things of luncheon
To be laid out on grass: the picnic rug,
The plates and glasses entirely like those
Captured so famously by that painterly eye
That depicted on canvas a lunch on grass,
Somewhere in sylvan France, sometime
In a less frenzied century, in surroundings bucolic.

With the accoutrements laid, the meal
And its attendant conversation may begin:
Lunch reveals the world and its implications
In the most generous of lights, amenable
To the agreement and company
That this meal, so generous and unnecessary,
Daily and predictably can vouchsafe.

SIESTA

(three p.m.)

Brief oblivion is the retiring god
Worshipped in these rituals
Of secluded somnolence; democratic,
The rules of admission:
All are entitled to a few hours
Removed from the cares
Of keeping things going;
For they have found this truth:
The world, once set on its course,
Seems to manage without us,
Does not need to be watched
All day: statesmen, brokers,
Bureaucrats of every stripe,
May simply say that they'll be back
Later in the afternoon; only pilots,
Divers, surgeons, watchers
Of flickering dials, must remain wakeful,
While fortunate others, horizontally,
Are altogether elsewhere.

REFLECTION
(six p.m.)

If six o'clock is a familiar watershed,
The end of a gentle slope rather than
The low point of a daily and headlong drop,
It is still a negotiable geography:
The afternoon is, for most of us,
Often just a little bit too long.

   An afternoon that ended at four,
Would, for those of average energy,
Probably be quite long enough,
And would be welcomed, I suspect,
By those who look forward
To a leisurely bath, a statutory gin,
And an early and digestible dinner;

   If days were shorter, such sybarites say,
They would be less troubled;
There is only so much damage
A determined busybody or despot
Can do in the rationed light of winter;
Generals with an eye to conquest
Are firm in their preference for summer,
And its long days of campaigning;
Winter reduces most human depredations,
With its shorter days and accelerated dusk.

   Yet calendars, and the days they serve,
Are ultimately adjustable to our needs:

Only a small and entirely local intervention
Transforms six into five, barely imperceptibly,
And thereafter into attainable four,
Leaving us with shorter afternoons,
Less crowded days, and a comfortable sense
Of not having to rush unduly what we have.

COCOA

(nine p.m.)

Sound is the advice of nurse and mother:
'A hot milky drink taken just before bed
May not be what you want, but you are wrong,
Just as you are about many things: troubles
Are rarely as bad after a mug of hot cocoa.'

The purveyors of such advice usually practise
Exactly what they preach, lead blameless lives,
And die, in their beds, in their nineties;
Those who spurn cocoa tend to be more troubled,
Think themselves above such anodynes,
Lead a boisterous social life, have hypertension;
Listen, then, to nurse and to mother,
There is a peace that comes with compliance:
In the arms of cocoa is sweet oblivion found.

On a September day in 2022 the world lost one of its best-known figures – a person who represented to many the ideal of duty. Many people, throughout the world, felt a strong sense of loss when this happened – and gratitude, too, for a life of service.

A SEPTEMBER DAY

When we lose from our accustomed world
Something that had been part of the map
By which we thought we might manage
To find a way along what seems like
An increasingly difficult path,
We know there is little point
In dwelling too long on the inevitability
That dictates that everything ends;
Yet knowing the way a story concludes
Doesn't make the actual ending
Any easier, nor transform to any extent
The way in which the playwright
Writes the concluding act, the final lines.

Our picture of the world we inhabit
Is made up of the daily and the familiar,
Of places that form the background
Of our ordinary lives, always present,
Like certain people we assume
Will not really have to leave us,
And then suddenly are no longer there,
And we notice their loss, as if the lights
Have been suddenly dimmed,
Or a clock that was ticking
Has fallen silent, its hands
Stopping at an arbitrary
And unremarkable time:
A moment when most of us

Were doing nothing special,
Before we were told that something
We knew must happen, has happened.

It is at such times that reaching
The end of the final act, the point
At which the stage curtain must fall,
We realise what it is that we miss
In the normal way we lead our lives;
And we look for things that are permanent,
And not glibly imitated, nor for sale:
Duty and kindness, old-fashioned virtues
That we should never have dreamed
We did not need, but without which
The play in which we all are actors
Will not end well; we see these qualities,
And understand, with sudden shock,
How much we need one another,
How much we want to do better
With our bruised and suffering world,
How much we want love, not selfishness,
To be the note to which the orchestra tunes,
The note taken up by the chorus, and sung
Loud enough to drown out all the other noise.

Occupations

In the nineteenth century a number of large firms were established to take advantage of the demand for opium in China. The opium trade, and the wars that it spawned, seem almost inconceivable to a modern sensibility, yet they happened, and it was not until the second decade of the twentieth century that the officially-tolerated export of opium from India to China was suppressed. The large-scale devastation of whole communities by opium consumption finds its modern equivalent in the appalling damage being wrought in the United States by drugs such as fentanyl, brought over the border from Mexico or manufactured in illegal laboratories within the country.

TRADING FIRM

See this great firm whose satisfactory building
Sits on the business-district corner, convincing
In its embodiment of carefully-managed capital,
All Ionian columns and larger doors
Than are strictly speaking necessary,
Whose reach is authoritatively described
In a unfaltering mission statement replete
With office locations; whose innocent desire
Is professed to be the bringing of profit
To those with whom it lives and trades,
Whose gifts to a slew of good causes
Are more than occasional.
                    This firm
Started a long time ago, run by brothers
And by the sons of brothers, bought raw opium
From poor farmers, packed it neatly
In wooden chests, passed it on, without shame,
To merchants with whom it had a long history;
Forced it on unlucky and defenceless China
In return for shimmering silks; such was trade
In those days, commemorated here,
In columns and old-established names,
In stone built on foundations of misery;
Respectability is not hard to achieve
In a species with such a strong desire
To forget the unhappy things it would forget.

A SYMPATHETIC DOCTOR

Her hands tell the story:
A childhood of wanting to look after
Wounded creatures, an injured bird,
Unable to fly, a doll whose arm
Has broken, letting stuffing out,
A bee sting on a friend's finger:
Little signs that pointed the way
To long years of medical school,
And endless hours on draughty wards,
And the committal to memory
Of anatomical diagrams and chemistry.

Surviving all that, perhaps because of that,
The sympathetic doctor lays gentle hands
Upon the ill; probes wounds of body
As well as mind, gently relieves
The things that need relieving, the pain
That comes with being human,
Fortifies by touch and reassuring glance
The soul within the fragile envelope
Of the vulnerable body, makes better,
Refrains from reproach or warning,
For we are all mortal, all weak
When tempted by the things we shouldn't do.

Doctors are probably made before they reach medical school, even
if medical school provides the final polish.

I have come across shepherds in Scotland who know the ancestry of individual sheep in their flock as well as they know their own. In Scotland, a shepherd who can recognise a sheep may be known as a *kenner* (from the Scots verb, to ken). A good shepherd, like so many country people, is likely to be perfectly satisfied with his or her lot, as this poem suggests.

THE SHEPHERD

Who knows his sheep by name, or almost,
Who remembers which ewe begat which lamb
And by which enthusiastic ram;

Whose constant companion is a dog,
To whom he calls out left and right
To herd the sheep and bring them tight

Into the drystone fank; this countryman
Is indifferent to wind and rain,
Loves the life he's lived, would live it all again.

Spies

&

Espionage

THE PRINCIPLES OF ESPIONAGE

This is a poem for those
Who have, in private moments,
Imagined what it might be like
To be a spy; an immature fantasy,
But common enough.

This is a hollow tree,
This is the place where, furtively,
A message may be dropped,
A microfiche of documents
Revealing who is planning
To do what: the movement
Of armies, the identity
Of those who, in clandestine circles,
Are called particular assets:
The language of dehumanisation
Is on every tongue here.

This is invisible ink in which
This poem is not written;
This is the way you i on the page
And see the coded message emerge,
This is what that looks like.

This is the place you wait for hours
To see if the person you're waiting for
Will arrive; this is the lamppost
In whose circle of light
The furtive figure will appear.

This is a moral dilemma;
This is what it looks like,
That indecision as to whether
A cause is greater, weightier
Than the loyalty you owe
To those who always thought
You belonged exclusively to them,
This is how disloyalty looks,
This is the face of betrayal;
Study it carefully before forgetting it.

This is a lonely bridge somewhere,
This is where you may have to cross
Into a life of silenced exile;
This is the undistinguished café
In which you will sit all alone;
This is what they call a safe house,
Which may not feel quite so safe.

These are the reasons, or some of them,
Why it might be wiser
To avoid the first step into night.

FIVE POEMS ABOUT FOUR SPIES

Who amongst us does not enjoy at least the occasional book about spies? An extraordinary amount of ink has been spilled over the so-called Cambridge spies, a group of friends who were recruited as agents by Soviet intelligence before the Second World War and who continued to work for Moscow in the post-war period. Their cover was, to an extent, the fact that they were members of the Establishment: few thought that people with their social credentials would betray their country. Some of them felt they had no alternative: that only Russia was prepared to stand up against the horrors of European fascism. They were probably ignorant, at an early stage, of the real nature of Stalin's rule; that excuse would have worn progressively thinner as the world learned of the Great Terror and its consequences.

I. CAMBRIDGE, 1932

This is a city in which more is meant than is expressed,
In which gesture is as important as declaration,
In which it would be as difficult to ignore
What is not said as that which is said;
Centuries here are implicit and uncelebrated;
The world may change but certain truths
Are constant, and require no new signpost;
This academic theatre exists for youth
With an expectation of rejection:
Each generation finds out afresh
What its parents consistently did wrong,
And then does the same thing itself;
Each generation believes its particular challenges
Are unique in their complexity, have never
Been faced before, nor spoken or written about.
Few people think that in spite of everything
They will do what people like them
Have always done and will continue to do.
This year was one of innocence:
The worst was to come, when unimaginable
Cruelty was given its head, and the concerns
Of this city, at this time, were made small
By the enormity of intended evil.

II. KIM PHILBY

Not particularly loved by a father
Who preferred Beirut and its society
To the early bedtime of England;
Left to work out for himself
How he might take a stand
On the great issues of the day,
He had no difficulty with that,
For he was serious in his choice,
In his rejection of the easy lie,
Or of widespread indifference
To the iniquities of a system
He had never really liked;
Since he saw no other way
To right the egregious wrong
He took that first step into another loyalty,
Not imagining for a moment
How it would end in Moscow
Years from now, with a military funeral
And a small attendance of lovers,
But with no reference being made
To anything beyond what is here, nothing;
Because the state, that provided
The apartment and the years of privilege,
Discouraged belief in the incredible;
Largely alone in his notoriety,
Living with numerous requests

For interviews and signs of regret,
The long-concealed secrets
Have been put away, gather dust,
Become history, rather than politics.

III. ANTHONY BLUNT

Knowing his French painter and every stroke
Of that neo-classical brush, quite capable
Of telling at a glance whether a provenance
Was nine parts hope, or more, as many are,
Able to quote what it is that makes a painting
An object of our wishful affection; bemused
By the grubbiness of life, rejecting
The *profanum vulgus* that Horace had dismissed,
Believing that treason was the only way
Of saving allies from slaughter,
Convinced that he was right, and that
History required him to do his duty,
Not one to cause the death of another, denying
That ever happened; increasingly lonely,
Dreading the moment of exposure
And the braying of the unlettered
Who knew nothing of why he once denied
He had ever done anything, although he clearly had.

IV. GUY BURGESS

Outrageous by any standards other than those
Of a drunken habitué of a disreputable bar,
He felt he had to challenge the harsh ways
Of those who had made his whole life wrong,
Who dictated that his private search for solace
Should be a casual crime. He hated
To see hunger and bullying; but still
Never cared to be anything very much
But outrageous and socially unacceptable,
A walking time-bomb who, careless in his goodbyes,
Drank himself enthusiastically to death
By another river altogether, far from home
Under a very different and a colder sky.

V. DONALD MACLEAN

At school he would have loved
Not to be subject to that awful code
Of individual honour; would have loved
Not to hide the way he truly felt
About fathers and Parliament;
Would have preferred to be able to share
The plan he and a few others
Had for stopping our own people
From planning our individual deaths;
He disliked the way people were so possessive
Of the bombs that could end it all;
He wanted a different distribution,
In which the megatons were shared equally
And all would be equally frightened:
Little to ask, he thought, little to ask.

Kim Philby: the real McCoy. He was no amateur, weekend spy – he was in it for the long run. He was a consummate liar, who brazened it out until eventually he had to escape. He passed on information that he knew would lead to the death of many resistance fighters landing in communist-controlled areas in the Balkans.

Anthony Blunt: He was an art historian who got caught up in the messy business of espionage. He was a highly cultivated expert on the French painter, Nicolas Poussin. I share his interest in Poussin, in spite of the undeniably cold nature of many of his paintings. Blunt was the director of the Courtauld Institute in London, and a number of my friends were students of his there. He was much admired by his students. He had a Poussin in his flat. He was outed by Margaret Thatcher, who did not like the Establishment bargain that led to Blunt being protected from prosecution. After he was exposed, he went one evening to a cinema in London and was recognised by members of the audience. He was slow-clapped out of the auditorium – a profound humiliation.

Guy Burgess: an outrageous drunk. Florid. A rebel who was created by the English boarding school system of his times – a distorter of young lives, if ever there was one. The emotional crippling that resulted from that system cast a long shadow.

Donald Maclean: He believed that if America had atomic weapons and the Soviet Union did not, World War Three was inevitable. He had very strong anti-American prejudices. He passed on atomic secrets because he felt it was his moral duty to do so.

Although one may understand the reasoning that propelled Blunt into espionage, in passing on important military intelligence to Soviet spy masters during the Second World War, Blunt could have compromised the surprise element of the Normandy landings. Soviet intelligence was heavily penetrated by Nazi spies, and anything that Blunt gave the Russians could have ended up in German hands. If the Allies had lost the element of surprise, the history of the world could have been very different.

Some years ago, I started to write a libretto for an opera about Anthony Blunt. It did not get very far, but I have kept what was written. One of the characters in it was Margaret Thatcher, who sings this aria. It ended up sounding a bit Gilbert-and-Sullivan-ish, but I can still picture – and hear – it being sung as a sort of *J'accuse*.

THE DENUNCIATORY ARIA

Sung by Margaret Thatcher, in Parliament (Act Three)

Mr Blunt did for the Soviet Union spy,
He betrayed us all, he betrayed us all,
And now the question asked is why
Should any man for the Soviet Union spy,
Should repay our trust with the practised lie,
With the practised lie, with the practised lie.

Mr Blunt to his masters in Moscow sends
Our secrets grave, our secrets grave,
Each one picked for his Communist friends
To use at will for nefarious ends,
The fabric of trust in this way rends,
Our State, and our trusting country offends.

I could not resist writing an aria for Mrs Thatcher, who was, in her way, very theatrical. She would have had a contralto voice in the opera, without a doubt. Here is another short excerpt, sung by the chorus in the first act:

NOW SPAIN LIES HELPLESS

Chorus – In the bar (Act One)

Now Spain lies helpless,
In the dark shadows
Of Europe's long-tormented night;
Bows, now humbled, to naked might.
While Spain so helpless lies

The ranting German
Toxic spells invokes
To bring to reawakened life
The buried gods of war and strife.
While Spain so helpless lies

A monstrous sickness
Infiltrates the soul;
Some ancient unforgotten cause
Historic insult, blood and force
While Spain so helpless lies

Rampant pride and hate,
In history's kitchen
A lethal potion will devise;
The patient now before them lies.

Appetites of the Soul

Love is an appetite of the soul; other appetites exist. The next two poems are about food; they are followed by one on the digestion.

Lin Yutang was a Chinese writer who enjoyed a wide readership in the west following the publication of his book, *My Country and My People*, in 1935. Another book of his, *The Importance of Living*, contains an extremely amusing whimsical essay on conditions that displease flowers. 'Flowers,' he said, 'do not like the sound of idle monks chattering. They like, however, the sight of young women attending to their hair.'

His comment on patriotism has been widely quoted. Like so many pithy aphorisms, it is only partly true.

THE THINGS WE ATE IN CHILDHOOD

Patriotism, said the essayist Lin Yutang,
Is nothing but the love of what we ate
As children – that is all he saw in it –
A reductionist view that those many others
Who hold their individual countries dearer
Than shared geography would dispute;
And yet it is still true that most of us
Still love the food of childhood years,
The taste of the simple things we ate,
And the way things smelled and looked
When we were children, all those years ago,
Which is what he really meant to say.

The childish palate is not given
To strong flavours and to sauces,
Bland and milky are the notes
That mark the nursery menu:
Fish boiled in milk, custard
Topped with raspberry jam,
Buttered bread with hard-boiled egg,
Or soggy cereal with a sugared crust,
Are settled features of a menu
That pleases those who have not yet
Learned to cook, or ask for something
Different and more challenging.

If Lin Yutang is proven right,
Then all that we will take to heart
Is a settled way of doing things,

And familiar ways of thinking;
Nothing else, no cause nor ambition
Will stir us to sing an anthem
Or a national song, no principle
Will raise an army, other than one
Conscripted and obliged,
And the defence of yesterday
Will be the cause that excites
The greatest enthusiasm;
Which, when we look about,
The stubborn conflicts of the world
Seems strangely true; few volunteers
Fight for a future, while rather many
Fight so fiercely for the past.

Scrambled eggs are not as easy to cook as some people think. There is a major difference between well-prepared scrambled eggs, and scrambled eggs that have been concocted with no regard to the ingredients, simple though they may be. Scrambled eggs should be cooked slowly, not rustled up in a few minutes. But can you change your mind once you have started to scramble the eggs? The folk wisdom suggests you cannot.

THE SCRAMBLING OF EGGS

They are both breakfast fare and metaphor;
As a meal they serve the immediate needs
Of the cooked offering that requires only
A few ingredients, and yet taste good enough
When comfort food is what we feel we need,
Rather than anything more complex and obscure.
   The eggs should be cooked slowly, though,
And with care, according to this recipe:
Stir the eggs, gently, as one might mix
A delicate concoction in a fragile bowl;
Avoid the use of milk, butter alone
Will achieve the consistency you desire;
Then add pepper, and salt to taste,
Transfer to buttered toast and serve at once.

To say, as people do, that eggs cannot
Be unscrambled, to make the point
That what is mixed cannot be unmixed,
Is wrong; a moment's thought reveals
That to unscramble eggs all one needs to do
Is to follow the steps above, but in reverse.

It is probably best not to see what happens to food once we swallow it. A chef may take great pains to present a dish in an attractive manner, with a decorated plate and the tasteful arrangement of accompaniments. But once the food is swallowed, it moves into democratic darkness and into the arms of the organisms that teem in our insides. We may not know their names, but without them we would perish. Their number is legion, but their achievements largely unsung.

Their civilisation is largely silent and well-behaved,
Aware, for the most part, that they are citizens
Within a larger polity, whose inner economy
Will determine their own future, they behave
With due consideration, performing the functions
Biology allocates, only occasionally do they riot,
Showing their displeasure at the uninvited presence
Of some culture of undesirables, toxic rowdies
Who muscle in on the coat-tails of an out-of-date pie
Or an imperfectly cooked curry; quite understandably
They object, reminding their host, sometimes forcefully,
Of their susceptibilities and fixed opinions.

   Otherwise, they are pacific, ready to serve, uncomplaining,
The sort of dinner companions we all would choose,
Asking little, on our side in any heated table-talk,
Conscious, too, of the fact that when all is said and done
They are guests, and should behave as such.
Without them, we cannot live, cannot digest;
Their essential culture is a macrobiotic sacrament;
Do not be too clean, they advise, in what you eat;
Never decline to replace on the plate
The things you inadvertently drop on the floor:
We like a challenge, they say: remember that.

Greece

The Ancient World

We live on an island; but then so does everybody else, although in some cases the island is rather large. Australia is an island, and yet Australians do not think of themselves as islanders. Perhaps what gives a place a sense of insularity is the need of those who live there to cross water to go anywhere else.

Islands have a particular charm. When we are on an island we are cut off from the rest of the world, and at times that may be exactly what we want. I travel regularly to small islands off the west coast of Scotland. I sail to Muck, Rum and Canna – three small and very beautiful islands just to the south of the Isle of Skye. I anchor and row ashore. Seabirds wheel across the sky; clouds sail past on the way in from the Atlantic; in the distance, if conditions are clear enough, I can just make out the Outer Hebrides – Barra and the Uists.

This poem was written after a visit to very different islands – the islands of the Ionian. While there, I read about some of the issues that have arisen between Ionian islanders and the authorities in Athens. That gave me cause to reflect on how islanders can have a long historical memory and a reserved, even suspicious, cast of mind. Many islanders resent, with good reason, being *fought over*. Their history is sometimes one of being used as parcels of real estate that can be given to others or sold to the highest bidder. Many islands have had more than their fair share of invasions – and understandably resent that distinction.

Islands often do not belong to people who think they should belong to them. There is no shortage of contested islands. Think of Rockall, the Falkland Islands, and so many others. There are also islands that are man-made in order to support a claim made to adjacent seabed. These arguments and rivalries could very easily result in humanity blowing itself up. No island is worth that. *Nothing* is worth that.

ON THE NATURE OF ISLANDS,
AND OF ISLANDERS

All islands, when given the chance, will protest
That the mainland, perhaps only a few miles away,
Is a quite other world, with an understanding
Very different in all its observable essentials
From that which prevails here, on insular soil,
With its pass-the-parcel constitutional experience:
   Islands, as history shows, make ideal gifts,
To cement an alliance between rulers
With an interest in dynastic security;
They serve, too, as a convenient excuse
For long disputes about who owns what:
Many a carefully nurtured *casus belli*
Is to do with ownership of recalcitrant land
That nobody really wants – not for itself;
Islands, in particular, perform that role rather well;
It does not matter very much that it is barren rock
That may be fought over – symbolism is what counts
When one people wishes to defeat another;
   The Senkaku Islands are home to none,
And not a place where any would wish to live;
And yet they may be quite enough
To make at least three fully-primed countries
Go enthusiastically to war, blowing our whole world up
By a side wind, by a strategic mistake.

Those who inhabit islands are often indifferent
To these arguments: their dislike may be even-handed,
Having as little taste for mountains as for plains,

And for any of the lures of a capital
In which attitudes and ambitions repel,
And that is unwilling, it seems, to pay attention;
    That, of course, is what all peripheral regions
Complain about: that those whose job
It is to hear them simply do not listen,
Just as the inebriate in the local bar
Bemoans to the perfect stranger on the next stool
His wife's impatience with his issues,
And is barely heard, and certainly not remembered;
    Like all discontents, no amount of attention
Will resolve the grievance; a separation of water
Will always mean that what is offered
Is not quite enough; yet even as they lament
The indifference of the mainland,
They remain glad that they are who they are,
And are, in their individual way, content;
Those who leave islands behind them
Frequently return, to live among others
Of the same constitution, with similar features
And bearers of recognisable island names,
With a shared past within them and a love
Of the simple, milky dishes of childhood;
Islanders, for all their posturing,
Are fundamentally content, fond of the sun,
Inured to rain, depending on latitude,
Unwilling to venture too far, to abandon
Being girt by sea, as geography has decreed.

IONIAN

The latitudes from which we, now as before,
Accustomed to altogether colder waters
And insistent rain, are repeatedly tempted,
Are northern ones; the familiar voice
We hear in the wind whispers *north*;
Our hills return an obedient echo;
North is their message, northern their faith,
Northern are the things they have for us to do.

And if, as is perhaps understandable,
We head south, part of an old progression
Of sun-worshippers, devotees of the pipes
Of innocent shepherds, devourers of figs
And local wine, both sold in markets –
Delighting in invitations of a gentler nature,
One receptive to olive trees and seas
That have too little room to be
Truly angry, then that is because
We are moved by another part of our psyche,
One that North herself has scolded
For being altogether and incorrigibly unsuited
To a landscape of hills and concealing mists
Appropriate to hills; of a landscape
That knows what lies in store for it
As early as September these days,
When summer makes its excuses
For its behaviour, and leaves us to it.

Not imagining that we could ever aspire
To fit as naturally into this world
As do the easy-living and unhurried residents,
Whose homes and villages are south of north,
Who may have forgotten their classical heritage,
But who are proud enough of it anyway,
We nonetheless try to bring to mind
Those bits that remain – the odd phrase,
The occasional memory of ancient gods
With whom we were once on nodding terms,
And who they were, although in a rational age
It is only too easy to get them mixed up
And attribute to one a temper tantrum
Or a sulk that really belonged to another.

Others have done the same,
Succumbed to the temptations
Of a beckoning south,
Famously so, in some cases,
Adopting a cause or subscribing
To a mood, a way of being,
As the Romantic poets did;
Byron answered the call
Of shores very similar to these;
He was not the last poet
To make the understandable mistake
Of getting uncomfortably close
To a particular sort of beauty;

We're wiser now: we understand
That mists, though charming,
May at the same time be miasmic.

Of course, those who go elsewhere
Have to return; home awaits,
And smiles at the old story
That South presented,
Says: these things are guiles,
But nevertheless do the trick, enable you
To survive a winter, ignore
The things you'd like to ignore,
By simply closing your eyes and
Seeing Ithaca again, and its sea,
And a shore of rounded stones,
Blue and white, washed smooth,
On which Odysseus himself
Set foot in coming home.

THE PERSISTENCE OF MYTH

If the old gods seem to be a long time dying,
It is because, as they told us often enough,
They are immortal – it's ordained, they say,
That they should still be around, never
Being obliged to exit the stage because the audience
Has become restless and has started to leave;
Mortals, of course, cannot overstay their welcome,
Being susceptible to so many conditions
For which nothing, or very little, can be done:
Age, for instance, or the eruption of volcanoes,
Or sudden and unexpected engineering failure;
There are so many ways we have to go,
Only a few of them considered pleasant.

    People understand how tenuous is our grip,
And how limited our human possibilities,
But still need an occasional sharp reminder
Of supernatural powers, of the awful effect
Of an intentional storm in which displays of lightning
Are not just for effect, flung to amuse the cheap seats;
Zeus, and those of his mind, were always more convincing
Than any pantomime villain of mortal invention,
And still are: sailors in Greece have never stopped
Treating Poseidon with the respect he is due, and Athena,
Some feel, is still there, ready to confer benefits
On the deserving few who are prepared to see her,
Rather than deny, as most of us do, that she exists.

But it is not only the immortal who survive:
A broad supporting cast of heroes is still remembered,
Occurs in our dreams, populates constellations,
Reminds us of what to avoid, what failings
To identify in others, what object lessons
To teach our children;
                        Cupid, unretired yet,
After aeons of mischief, still keeps his bow at the ready,
Smiles from contemporary greeting cards,
Allows his image to decorate unambiguously
The lonely-hearts columns of the newspapers,
Has a success rate well beyond chance;
    Tantalus and Sisyphus, unfortunate in their predicament,
Still echo in the words we use to frighten ourselves,
When even the gutsy terms of Anglo-Saxon
Are not up to it, may be too tame
To describe what an ill-tempered deity has done.

Of course, when it comes to the truly grand theme,
To the story that all of us feel reflects so very personally
The allegorical journey that we take our life to be,
Nothing, it seems, has been written remotely
To match that protracted and hazardous voyage
Back to Ithaca; for, if there is a destination
We all yearn for, still, after all that has happened,
It is that small island, peaceful with thyme and hills;
If there are waves whose breaking comforts
All but the most insomniac and most troubled of us,
It is those that wash Ionian shores; it is those sounds
We all hear as we close our eyes on the familiar,
As we await our homecoming, and our sleep.

Centaurs were an unruly bunch with the energy and strength of the horse, even if they had some of the intelligence of man. In this poem about the Argonauts, Chiron, the wisest of the Centaurs, comes out well, which is not surprising, as he was by far the best of that bunch.

The Argonaut story, of course, is universally and perpetually appealing. Men still dream of going off on a boat with a few friends, free from the restraints and anxieties of land. That is one of the reasons why Patrick O'Brian is so popular as a novelist: Jack Aubrey and Stephen Maturin do just that. Indeed, O'Brian himself invented a false past for himself in which he went off to sea with a friend while still in his teens, something that never happened.

Chiron ran a school on the flanks of Mount Pelion. It was a boarding school for boys: in those days, parents were quite happy to entrust their offspring to a headmaster who happened to be half horse. A charismatic principal always helps a school to succeed.

I. ARGONAUTS

A tutor should be wise, slightly distant perhaps,
Standing apart from those whose futures
He has been paid to fashion, whose instruction
In ways thought fitting and productive
Is the whole point of the arrangement;
    No false equality, then, no first-name terms,
At least in those cultures where, quite naturally,
Formal terms of address are readily available
And sound neither pompous, nor archaic;
The perfect balance between familiarity
And unwarranted reserve is not something
They can instil at the average teaching college,
It comes, if it comes at all, like good deportment
And ability to throw a ball or return a serve,
With practice, and with some contribution
From inherent talent:
              You either have it
Or you don't – it's innate, perhaps –
But when it's there, there's no mistaking it:
Students instinctively know a natural teacher
When they meet one in a lecture theatre,
Even if the college authorities, bureaucrats all,
Would never give Socrates tenure or a chair.

So, wise Chiron had probably never been taught
How to instruct youth; he belonged
To an unpredictable and headstrong crowd:
Centaurs, half-horse, half-man, skittish
Descendants of a cloud and an unreliable king,

Are a passionate tribe, unable to hold their drink,
Only too ready to lose control
    And stampede off in a dangerous direction;
Their credit ratings are poor, their reputation
For doing the wrong thing well-founded;
Their presence at a wedding guaranteed
To end in disorder and a fist-fight;
Normally, a centaur would be the last person
You'd choose to run a boarding school
Or invest a trust fund with prudence;
Yet Chiron had a reputation
For doing just those things, and more.

On his mountainside, sweet with thyme,
With Pelion's peak half-veiled behind him,
He hardly needed to advertise
His academic groves; word travels quickly
Amongst parents anxious that their offspring
Should get the best possible education,
To equip them for the frequently demanding
Task of living in classical Greece,
And for roles imposed by parentage:
To be the child of a god and a sea-nymph,
Or of a young woman seduced by a passing shadow,
Meant that destiny had marked you out,
And you would need some esoteric knowledge
As well as such supplies of native cunning
As fortunate breeding had provided.

    Who better than one who had seen
Rather a lot of human affairs from the perspective

Of those who do not quite belong,
Being half-horse and half-man,
Endowed with human reason, but capable
Of understanding the insistent need
That a quadruped feels to do things
According to a very different nature?

Wise Chiron said:
    Bring the boys
To my academy, here on this mountain,
And I shall return them to you
As men, capable of acquitting themselves
With distinction in any mythology,
Without any of the doubts that go
With knowing more than you should;
Enlist them here: none will be turned away,
And bear in mind I am immortal
And therefore will not do as some professors do
And die before the students sit their finals.

They came, shy, hopeful, reluctant, cocksure some,
The offspring of comfortable parents,
Some of whom were gods, while others
Had small kingdoms, each vaguely related
Because of the ways of prominent Greeks;
 Generations passed through Chiron's hands,
Sons returning to study what their fathers learned,
Using his bow, his handed-down spears, perhaps,
And such of his textbooks and lecture notes
That were not too out-of-date, nor withdrawn
For being unsuitable to an age of heroes.

Jason was enrolled; he had experienced
A bad start; internecine strife, envies, blighted
The beginnings of so many lives in those times,
And had made his beginning an example
Of how not to found emotional security;
He was entrusted to the care of Chiron
At a tender age, and would stay
Until he was clearly ready to move on
To heroism and its endless quests;
There is something touching about the story
Of any child who is sent to school
When things have become disastrous at home,
And who finds there the things
His young life has so far lacked:
Friendship, and the things that friendship brings.

And such playmates! Achilles, Heracles, and Asclepius,
All names that would resound
On those, and other shores,
But then just boys, doing the things
That boys will do when on a mountainside,
Each pursuing the gifts that wise Chiron
Saw in each of them and encouraged:
  The best of teachers is always the one
Who cultivates what's already there,
Embellishes it, gives it a name.

And so Achilles was shown the ways
Of weapons; much later, he would be thankful
For this early education, when before their tents
He and Patroclus would stand together

While missiles shot about their ears;
And Heracles, too, would be relieved
That Chiron had insisted on several hours
In the gymnasium each day, lifting trees,
Tossing rocks about as we throw
Crumpled paper;
                    and Asclepius, gentler
Than the others, would be shown the herbs
That made up his particular armamentarium,
Ready to bring relief to pain, reduction of fever,
Sleep to the sleepless, and release.

Jason, Chiron pronounced, you have far to go,
And in your going be polite,
Speak courteously to all you meet,
And defend the right.
   Jason nodded – he was not sure
What Chiron meant, but understood
That predictions, in those days, though Delphic,
Had an uncanny way of coming true,
And then at last one knew just what they meant.

In quiet friendship the youths would gather
And listen to old Chiron, who played the harp
Better than most, sing of things he had seen,
Of fields and seas and rivers, of the ways
Of creatures, real and only to be imagined,
And of how the gods played with those
Who angered them, and sought revenge,
And how they might be appeased
By a timely sacrifice that sent sweet smoke

Heavenwards for their propitiation,
All things those boys needed to know.

And by themselves they ran and sang and dived
Into mountain streams, shot deer with arrows
Fashioned in bone, watched circling eagles warily,
Knowing that one could well be Zeus
Looking for another Ganymede:
Watch out, boys, warned Chiron.

At length, Chiron took Jason aside:
You have been happy here, I can tell,
But the happiness of boyhood
Is not for ever; now you must go
Back to your nasty step-uncle,
And see what you can do
To get back what is yours: good luck!
If childhood is a paradise, it is one
From which we know we shall be excluded;
That's what gives any paradise we can imagine
Its special appeal, what makes it different
From the ordinary world outside;
I'll be sorry to see you go, as will be your friends,
But they and you will unite again quite soon,
And undertake a voyage, I believe.

II. QUEST

They seem to accept it, these heroes,
The quest on which they are sent,
Even though, at times, the burden
Surely must be hard to bear;
Nobody is perfect, even the strongest,
And the ostensibly exceptional,
Endowed with such strength and talent
As to make the other fellows look weak;
Even he might be forgiven for wondering
Why the gods elected him, in person,
To perform such an implausible task;
After his fourth labour, Heracles,
Though uncomplaining, might ask
How many more lay ahead,
And why these might not be shared
With those with rather less to do,
And even more eager to be given
The chance to shine, the opportunity
To appear, triumphant, on the front page
Of the newspaper they all read at home.

    Chance might have been kinder, given others
More of a look-in, but she picked him
And her election must be respected:
There may be quests in profusion,
But never quite enough to go round.
Because he understood this, Jason
Did not say *Why me?* but accepted
It was his lot to build a boat and travel
In quest of something somewhat unlikely,

Hanging on a tree in a distant
And unfriendly place: all he knew
Was that this was typical quest material,
And he would have to go, though not alone:
Every quest is enlivened, made more sociable,
By the addition of stalwart friends;
I'm off on a quest he wrote, *any interest*
In coming along with me? Quick the replies,
Sent by sure-footed and express messengers:
Count me in, of course: You're on!
And so a crew list of hopefuls emerges,
And each name is synonymous with courage.
'Now all I need,' says Jason, 'is a boat,
For I am fortunate in one thing at least:
I know what I'm looking for –
Can you, may I ask, say that?'

III. THE BUILDING OF A BOAT

Any competent carpenter can build a boat,
But few, it seems, will create
A craft capable of gladdening the hearts
Of the old men sitting in harbour cafés,
Stern critics each, enjoying the sun,
Which is free, predictable, and even-handed,
Grumbling about the Government,
But certain of what they like in a boat,
Appreciating the elegance of a good sheer
And a stern that allows the water
A swift recovery; Argus, of course.
Understood all that, his contract books
Were full until December, and beyond,
His clients numerous, the stories about him
Universally complimentary. 'A boat?
Of course I can, and will begin right now,
For this, I sense, is a voyage
That cannot wait, and must be undertaken.'
Jason said: 'It is, and must. And we shall call it the Argo,
In recognition of its maker.' And Argus, pleased, began.

IV. ACROSS THE SEA

The wind was favourable and the sea was blue;
Blue to us, that is, who are imagining it now,
But not necessarily to Jason and his crew;
They, just as we do, thought the things about them
Were what they believed them to be:
Not everybody sees blue the same way;
And some might simply have been indifferent
To the whole idea of blueness;
Or it is possible that the Greeks thought
Of light and dark, of shade and shadow,
Rather than of blue, or silver, or turquoise:
That is clearly one way of looking at the world,
And would explain why Homer
Famously talks of the wine-dark sea;
Since then, scholars have debated
What he meant, but have reached no conclusion;
For sailors, it is not colour, nor even shade,
But roughness and stillness that count;
    We choose the things we need
To say something about, and may ignore the rest;
May say little about the colour of the sea,
Fail to remark on something so familiar,
On things that, simply, are always there,
And that will persist to do the things they do,
With whatever words, and in what tone
We describe the way they look, the way they are.

Poems on Nature

THE FEEDING OF BIRDS

A flock of common pigeons, unrelated
To the garden birds we would prefer
To grace our free and tiny banquet –
Wagtails, goldfinches, those unlikely
Flashes of gesture or colour
That complement the in-bred flowers,
Intriguing shrubs, ornamental grass –
Feeds now on appropriated grain
Renewed again by daily miracle.

We cannot dictate the birds
Who will frequent our gardens;
Descending to entertain an audience
They would prefer not to be there,
Indifferent to our preferences
For this species over that;
Ornithology, you see, is ecumenical,
Discourages the cautious and canonical
Exclusion of lesser and unpopular birds:
The air and its creatures, in spite of us,
Make up a rough democracy,
Citizens of somewhere, of an aerial city.

No bird questions where the free meal
Comes from, for them this bounty,
Appearing daily, is just part of a world
That is there and always has been;
So, too, do we rarely bother to ask
How it came to be that we should enjoy

The primate ascendancy we have created,
That reassures us in our confident
Possession of a perfect right
To be what we are, in a world we define,
Rarely comparing ourselves in any way
To the less fortunate species
Disappearing daily, one by one,
Into an extinction caused by us;
To those entirely unlike ourselves:
Small, feathered creatures, innocent each,
Untroubled by our particular burden,
Which is that fundamental question
They've never had to ask, giving them time
To sing without script, fly through
Air whose purpose it is to support them,
Needing no Latin to know who they are,
Indifferent to philosophy, unneedful of guilt.

WOLF INTO DOG
How it all began, and continues

Wary of our missiles, stick and stone,
Having noticed from a fair distance
The sure effect of a well-aimed rock
On the half-felled boar, the cornered deer,
Tempted by the inviting smell of roasts,
The hungry wolves nightly edged closer
To the messy encampments and fires
Of our hirsute and footloose forebears,
Concluding, these wily carnivores,
That it might make reasonable sense
To forge a loosely-worded treaty,
A species contract, one in which they,
The sharp-toothed ones, wolfkind, the fleet,
Would help to bring down a common prey
In return for scraps we sent their way.

Domestication is the best word
To describe this practical compact;
And canine, the category into which
We'd put these early, pragmatic wolves
Now defined as dogs; they would become
Aware in time that sheer loyalty
Would dictate what they would feel for us
And what we'd admire in turn in them;
Though, by then, it would be far too late
To scrap a clearly unequal bond –
Independence is never easy

When others control the food supply:
A lesson every polity learns.

Far better, then, to submit at last
To a regime of belittling names,
To restrictive collars and short chains,
And the occasional glimpse of glory:
Portrayed in an old Roman fresco
Or a Flemish tapestry that placed
Hunting dogs lying at hunters' feet,
A mention in some sentimental
Lines of poetry and prose, not viewed
Too seriously, but loved by all,
By trusting children and policemen
Who instruct them in the sniffing out
Of contraband, of analgesic
Leaf and all its seductive powders,
Who train them to growl at intruders
For whom a dog would feel equal love,
Not knowing by what criteria
Are the human hunted distinguished
From human hunters; both dog and man
Have forgotten how this came about,
Cannot recall the smoky campfires
Around which so long ago we met,
Yet they still watch us with those trusting eyes,
Happier with human company
Than we perhaps deserve, forgiving
All, starting each day without thinking
Of what happened yesterday, content

To be beside us, in our shadow,
Bemused, though, at our indifference
To the olfactory, and our inexplicable ways.

Around the World

The calendar is now littered with special days marking some cause or issue. Some of these reflect local, and even commercial concerns, as is the case with World Whisky Day (the third Saturday of each May) on which people are urged to drink whisky at public events. Not everyone would approve of that, but the Scottish Parliament, in two separate motions, recognised that day. International recognition of named days is given by the United Nations, which nods in this way to a whole raft of causes. There is a Sustainable Gastronomy Day (18 June), a World Tourism Day (27 September) (perhaps one should avoid travel on that day) and many other world days. The public diary is now as crowded as that of an overworked dentist. The proliferation of these days possibly weakens their impact, but they are a useful way of reminding the public of particular issues that might otherwise be drowned out in the noise of everyday life. Of course, for a long time there have been saints' days. In Scotland we still celebrate St Andrew's Day each year on the 30th November with dinners and other events.

Not so much attention is paid to the feast day of St Joseph of Cupertino (18 September), a Franciscan friar who was said to have levitated in ecstasy, sometimes travelling considerable distances before returning to earth. Not surprisingly, he is the patron saint of air travellers. He was not an intellectually distinguished man, and indeed had difficulty satisfying his Order as to his ability to be a monk. Yet he persisted, as those intent on a career may do, and public support ensured his acceptance by the Order.

JOSEPH OF CUPERTINO,
EARLY AIRMAN

Failing to pass the unavoidable interview
That winnowed out the weaker and unlettered,
He made up for it, in the view of the people,
By being enthusiastic, as frauds and visionaries
Often are, although some who see things
That are patently not there, do so in good faith,
And with no intention to deceive.

Those like him, simple but unmissable
In demeanour and lack of complication,
Often give precisely what the people seek:
Indifferent to theologians telling them
About things they would never understand
And do not much care for, the masses choose
Those who speak an easier language altogether;
It's far better to have a simple friar,
A figure of fun, a holy fool, or just about,
Who leaps and shouts and makes a noise,
Rather than a clever man with a sharp tongue;
   The people are receptive, and always have been,
To the believable simpleton who claims
There is something beyond the things we see,
That's all, who sees a better tomorrow
Beyond the here and now, that is
So burdensomely here and now.

Religion is so much at once: a spiritual balm,
An inspiration for good works, for a life

Of service in a leper colony somewhere;
A way of allowing the sad at heart
To make amends for the things they've done;
It is also a tawdry brew of smoke and mirrors:
Levitating monks, liquefying blood
In Baroque reliquaries, or long damnation
Uttered by ranting preachers
In the unconditioned, Protestant air
Of wooden churches under the sun.
It is all those, as well as being a levitating man
To whom some still whisper their requests
At take-off time, or in the clouds,
Who lived before the jet engine
But who, I think, would have loved it so,
Forgiven it for what it does to the sky,
Delighted in the fact of flight and speed;
    Yet even as we think of him, that genial monk,
We remind ourselves once more of brutal fact:
We are born on land with rooted feet,
That we cannot fly is our earthly truth.

Sweden plays an important part in people's imagination. It is, for many, a beacon of social democracy – an enlightened state in which people behave rationally. Sweden is indeed different, but it now has a dark side that bubbles away under the cool exterior. Yet it is still a place that I find exhilarating to visit.

IN SWEDEN

Don't expect the trees to stop,
And the forests to apologise
For their monotonous horizons;
Don't wait for the sky to close in
To accommodate a narrower outlook;
Don't expect the white nights of summer
To darken, the blues to attenuate;
Don't tell yourself this is only
The beginning of a country rather than
A country itself: don't expect Sweden
To become more like everywhere else,
Or develop the bad habits that persist
In the places of a warmer south,
With their comfortable understandings,
Their Madonnas and their miracles;
That will not happen here,
In these woods, under this sky,
Amongst these people, confident
In their correct lives, endowed
With a collective good conscience,
Remembering a history of winter
And the survival of months of snow,
Of darkness, and ancient wooden boats,
And cured fish, and silences.

On one of my recent trips to Sweden, I travelled through Helsinki. I made this journey four months or so after the Russian invasion of Ukraine. As we came down over the flat Finnish landscape, I looked out of the window into the distance, to where Russia lay. This poem came to me there, on the plane.

LANDING AT HELSINKI
After More Than One Hundred Days of a War

Down to a table top of green
An invisible beacon guides our landing,
A disembodied voice calls the altitude;
The air is fresh and northern here,
Disturbed only by the heavy breathing
Of neighbouring ambition,
A landscape of ordered buildings
And rational highways is reassuring
But provides no protection against
An empire in irredentist mode;
Peter the Great may have lived
Three hundred years ago, or more,
But the old tricks of that culture,
The poisonings and the disappearances,
Have remained at hand in the dark cupboard
Of Russian statecraft: all that is not far away,
A few hours by road through dark forests
That have witnessed all this before:
Nothing changes, say the trees, we should know
Because what you see is what
Has always been and is no different;
Do not expect happiness, warn the birds,
Because if we ourselves sing it is only because
People expect us to, and we know no other way.

I would like to think it's easy
To become Finnish – a choice
Like so many others – what to wear,
On which warm island to spend
Two weeks of summer; what book
To read after the one following the next;
And yet, I'm told it is inordinately hard
To express yourself in a language
With fifteen cases; you cannot sound Finnish,
You have to be Finnish, and that is different;
Just as you cannot be Scottish until
You know just how to look
When complaining about Scottish history
And the injustices of the past,
Or when, standing on a strip of machair,
You look out towards the green sea
And manage not to weep.

And then, on another trip to Sweden, a few months later, I travelled via Amsterdam. This poem is concerned with the difference between northern and southern Europe. Not only is the topography different; so too is the mindset.

The reference to a samovar is to those strange heating apparatuses that you see in the galleys of planes. They disgorge hot water as required for the passengers' tea and coffee. To call them samovars seems not unreasonable.

FLYING FROM AMSTERDAM TO
STOCKHOLM

Our little Dutch plane with its samovar
And its courtesies; its enquiries as to whether
Everyone is comfortable – and they are –
Skims obediently and lightly
Over a layer of cumulus cloud;
The Netherlands, its tulip fields,
Its canals and collections of still lifes
By a hundred seventeenth-century hands,
Lies behind us; Scandinavia and north
Are our destination today, its plains
Bordered by snow and Russia,
Its forests still dark in our imagination,
Still concealing wolves that watch
Through yellow eyes; who wait
For the pace of their prey to falter;
I don't know whether I'm a creature
Of this world, or that, all I know
Is that the attenuated light of north
Makes me wish for a softer life,
A nature more tolerant of our creature needs,
For heat and butterflies and the bells
Of goats returning to the fold.

On two occasions, I lived for some months in Dallas. It is an extremely elegant city with a good conceit of itself. It has a certain style, as exemplified by a car I once saw draw up at a social occasion. It was a very expensive-looking vehicle and its number plate was unabashed. It read: C MYCAR.

My late Dallas friend, Marvin Sloman, made celebrated margaritas, that he served in glasses with salt-encrusted rims. I associate Dallas with those; with a diner called Bubba's, with its lipstick-pink benches and its comfort food; with the city's glittering skyline; and with its strong sense of a Texas hinterland that goes on seemingly for ever.

A few miles from where I lived was Love Field Airport where, on that fateful day in 1963, President John F. Kennedy landed and set off in his motorcade. There is still a slightly haunted air to that part of downtown Dallas where his car moved past the famous grassy knoll and history was changed with a few cruel shots. That incident still hangs about the city's name, a reminder of something dark and dreadful.

In Dallas I took saxophone lessons with an African-American musician, a great man and a fine jazz player, who ran an instrument repair shop. He was very kind to me, and sold me a number of saxophones – one made by Adolph Sax's studio, and another a beautiful French bass saxophone that, being too heavy to hold, came with a tripod stand. Richard Thomas said of his client who wanted to sell the saxophone: 'The cat who owns that horn wants to sell it.' The cat was no *felis domesticus*.

I taught at one of the universities there. My students, an agreeable group, invited me to play poker with them one evening. They knew I couldn't play, but there is a great tradition in America of taking money off an innocent who wanders into a poker game. They limited my losses to just under fifty dollars, which was very considerate of them.

DALLAS

The comfortable cars glide past,
Unhurried in a city where few turns
Are required to make one's way
Across the miles of Texas plain
Upon which this glittering
Place is built; you cannot see here
The things that fund this party:
The dusty cattle are distant,
The sluggish oil is subterranean;
This is a city of elegant clothing
And optimistic cheerleaders,
Not a place for misery or doubt.

   And if the sky should be too wide
And the summers seem a bit too hot,
Expensive children still play in the garden,
Iced tea is still served by household help
From somewhere altogether different,
A glittering opera entertains,
Talks are given, transactions sealed,
Margaritas mixed, chicken fried.

How different is Italy. I studied years ago at the University of Siena, and it was while I was there that I first visited Montalcino, one of those exquisite and dream-like hill towns that make the Italian landscape so enticing. Montalcino was much smaller in those days than it is today – and sleepier too. There was one hotel then, the *Albergo il Giglio*, and one *pensione* in one of the village squares. In that square there was a fountain and surrounding pool inhabited by some long-suffering goldfish. In the late afternoon each day, a group of small boys would walk past the pool and throw stones at the fish. This seemed to be some sort of ritual and it's possible that the fish accepted it as being an inevitable concomitant of being a fish in a small village in the Sienese hills.

I set my novel *My Italian Bulldozer* in Montalcino. The hero in that book travels to Italy and, being unable to find a car to hire, ends up hiring a bulldozer, which he drives to Montalcino. There he sees an interesting side to the local wine industry – Montalcino is justifiably proud of its famous wine, *Brunello di Montalcino*.

MONTALCINO

Loyal to a nearby republic,
To a black-and-white striped cathedral,
And a horse race run in a piazza,
With banners and blessings;
Unimpressed by larger neighbours
And their dreams of aggrandisement,
They retreated to this particular hill,
With its circular view of hostile activities
On the plains below, and were content
With the small comforts of a local cuisine
And a hillside of protective oaks,
On which a traditional summer boar hunt
Brought people out with their excitable dogs
And for the feast that followed pursuit.

Then came the discovery of the brown wine
They had until then taken for granted,
And the reception of pilgrims
Of a different sort, and from further away,
Who liked the small-scale and the quiet,
And the smell of woodsmoke hanging
In the air, and mushrooms foraged
Within sight of watchful town walls,
And a world where everybody
Was related to and understanding
Of those who lived a single beck away,
And determined, for reasons of loyalty,
Never to seek another home, never to say goodbye.

The Italian countryside was designed by nature to be the background to a pastoral dream. To live in that countryside – perhaps to grow olives or raise sheep – is a dream entertained by many people fed up with the urban rat race. Some of them may be influenced by Horace, the bucolic Roman poet who wrote about his Sabine farm and the joys of living a simple rural life. The Horatian theme has often been take up by other poets. Horace has that rare distinction, given to few writers, of having an adjective minted to their world or their philosophy. This happened to Marcel Proust (Proustian), Somerset Maugham (Maughamesque), Charles Dickens (Dickensian), and, of course, Homer (Homeric). Graham Greene, who specialised in milieux that are somewhat rundown and off-the-beaten-track, had the particular distinction of having a literary landscape named after him – *Greeneland*. I have occasionally found myself in that landscape – in a small hotel somewhere tropical and remote, where brown Windsor soup, with ancient croutons, is still served at tables covered with starched white tablecloths. Time, they say, does not stand still; in some places, though, it appears to do just that, and there the shade of Greene may briefly be glimpsed. In fact, *Fifty Shades of Greene* would be an apt title for a book that explored such lost and atmospheric places.

ON BEING HORATIAN

Tired of the city, but still watching
The ways of Rome, of the sophisticates;
Ready to play the once-fêted poet
Who secretly preferred rustic pursuits
And Falernian wine to those expensive vintages
Sold to the wine snobs and the parvenus;
A farmer, in appearance at least,
With all the right complaints
Up his country sleeve, ready to praise
A wealthy patron and an emperor,
In the voice appropriate to each,
Horace takes to his Sabine retreat,
Writes verses for those who wish
Their daily lives were simpler,
Sends his lines to an accustomed scribe,
Counts the return of sure-footed goats,
Becomes an adjective.

When I am in Oxford, I enjoy sitting in cafés in Jericho. The conversations that one cannot help but overhear are particularly interesting there.

Oxford, of course, is a city very closely associated with the life of the mind, and particularly with the teaching of philosophy, one of my special interests. This poem raises the problem of free will – something that undoubtedly concerns more than a few philosophers in Oxford. It may be difficult to defend free will from a theoretical point of view, but ultimately we have to live our lives as if it exists. A belief in determinism is incompatible with any notion of responsibility to which people would, in the conduct of their daily lives, respond. That is the issue discussed in this poem, that was written after a walk across Port Meadow, in the shadow of the then only recently lifted pandemic lockdown. I remember the emptiness of the sky, as air travel had yet to begin again, and there were none of the white vapour trails that normally criss-cross the blue.

I. THOUGHTS ON FREE WILL IN OXFORD

In Oxford now where, with some reluctance,
A late-to-arrive summer brings swimmers
To their favoured pool on the river,
And the grass on Port Meadow is patient
And determined to continue in spite
Of the discouragement of dry months
Of anticipation; there, below a sky
That is broad and empty, washed-out blue,
Relieved, by unexpected human disaster,
Of the criss-cross trails of those travellers
Who think nothing of the Alps or the Atlantic,
But who are grounded now, confined
To the local and more natural distances;
Innocent, a wind from somewhere further south
Makes the willows move, delicately,
Still a safe haven for the sweet and silent dove
That lands so suddenly upon a branch
And peers down, with that jerky movement of the head
That doves will make, and sees us, and is surprised.

    For whom free will is not an issue;
For most things that move about and breathe
Do so to the rhythm of their clockwork promptings;
Doves have never done much more
Than this dove does, have not questioned
Nor been unsure – straight are the tracks
Of determinism and avian nature,
Familiar the view, unvaried the song.
    So, too, have we gravitated to water,

[152]

As these swimmers do in the slow-moving river,
So, too, have we obeyed the instruction
To secure a biological future, as do the lovers
Who hand in hand, walk from this place
To the sanctuary of an unkempt student flat,
A place of posters and unwashed coffee cups;
We flatter ourselves, though, in imagining
That we, alone, make the only choices that count.
    And yet, if we did not delude ourselves,
If we did not believe that we could choose,
None of this would have been possible;
There would have been no Oxford, no gates,
No colleges, nor quiet conversations;
There would be no works of science
Nor books on butterflies or mathematics,
Because there would be no blame nor credit
For anything that we thought we chose.
The unapologetic dictator and the bully,
The selfish hoarder, the profligate and the spoiler,
Would be exonerated and without blame,
Because their past made them do the things they did;
The consequences would still matter to those
Who bore the brunt of these acts of fate,
But a shrug would be enough to signal
The inevitability of their pain or disappointment.
There would be no prizes, nor applause,
Because credit, if it still made sense,
Would go to nobody in particular:
Why begin a masterpiece, a painting
To express the world, when all along
The work of art has been destined

To be painted precisely as you planned it?
There is no challenge in painting by numbers
Says the non-reductionist critic.

In the street, a shout – a bicycle has been stolen;
The owner accepts the sympathy of others,
Nobody states the obvious truth:
That particular bicycle was stolen a long time ago,
Before it was made, before bicycles were invented,
Even before an ill-tempered Cain did *not* choose
To dispose of his inconvenient brother.
Somewhere, not far away, from a window in a quad,
A philosopher looks on, and thinks:
Perhaps we have to convince ourselves to believe
That which simply cannot be true;
Perhaps we have to defend free will
Because there is no other choice, just that.

Oxford is a city that has taken hundreds of years to create. You could never create such a place from scratch today. Enclaves of recently built neo-Georgian enclaves, insulated according to the latest standards, and served by fibre-optic cable, are incorrigibly pastiche. What the modern house built in the old style lacks is a patina that only comes with years of exposure to the elements and centuries of human mistakes. Human tears, human fears, give character to the buildings we inhabit.

II. IT HAPPENS

Most streets reflect the ordinary concerns of place;
Here, in a suburb of warm-brick houses, in Oxford,
Occurs Aristotle Lane, climbing a small bridge
Over a green and somnolent canal, quite natural
In its easy and classical assumptions;
Old names carry with them references
Nobody thought it necessary to explain,
Quirky, local, somehow typical
Of a city whose parish is still the world,
That has done so much to promote
Our understanding of who we are
And why we think the way we do,
And done it generously, in the belief
That knowledge belongs to nobody
In particular, is there for all,
And should make none feel uncomfortable;
A city that has nonetheless not forgotten
Its quiet corners, its nostalgic meadows,
Its predictable bells, its bicycles;
You can't invent a place like this – it happens.

In a Jericho café, fortunate with its walled garden,
In which vines have somehow been persuaded
To grow, as if much further south,
Improbable people – or improbable elsewhere,
But entirely natural and domesticated here –
Talk about matters philosophical;
Two retired tutors, from a college somewhere,
One the author of a book on the notion of the self,

The other a woman who finds the crossword far too easy,
Talk as their coffee grows cold;
One asks: what is the colour blue – does it exist?
'Not in any definitive sense,' her friend replies,
'Blue is what you think you see.'
She adjusts her scarf – it's blue –
And looks up at a sky that is attenuated blue,
Or at least that is what it seems to be;
While on the other side of the wall, unseen,
Two undergraduates, new in love,
Speak of a dinner that they plan to have:
A Chinese meal, always a test, one says,
Of whether he suits her, or the other way round;
They laugh; they do not realise how serious
Are the mistakes they'll make in life.
The women pause their talk of blue, and smile,
You can't create a mood like this – it happens.

Almost noon, in early October, autumn,
With all that autumn brings, although this year
It is still warm, even now, and leaves
Hang on tenaciously, in denial, I think;
I read somewhere, in some forgotten poem,
Of how vine leaves rattle like dice when brown;
Perhaps they do, although you'll need
To catch them at just the right moment
If you are to eavesdrop on their conversation;
It's a common desire, to stop the clock,
Especially when we are happy,
At such times it would be good, we feel,
To eke contentment out, to make it last;

I would spend my time, I suppose,
With old friends who stayed
Exactly as they were when I first met them;
I would frequent places that remained
Unchanged from how they were
When I first discovered them, well before
The guide-books came along;
I still hope my favourite authors and painters
Will escape re-assessment by spoilsports;
Now it's noon, and the shadows are as short
As they ever will be at this latitude, at this time:
You can't plan for sunlight to fall like this – it happens.

Robert Burns is Scotland's national poet for a very good reason: if there is a Scottish character, then it is represented in Burns. It is that simple. And he is relevant, still, after two and a quarter centuries. This poem was first published in *The Scotsman* newspaper in a Burns commemoration.

MISSING YOU ALREADY

What's two hundred and twenty-five years
In any full-blooded scale of things?
Not all that much really, not much –
What is written yesterday could so easily
Have been committed to paper today,
Only the grammar changes, slightly,
While the sentiment is exactly
What we continue to feel within,
Here in Scotland, where you once lived
And are remembered with pride.

There are some who still hold,
Against all the literary evidence,
That poets compose their individual lines
Detached from the insistent influence
Of what was written before their time;
That most poems are new, or almost new
Is a proposition that is not true at all:
Every poet has a private hinterland,
Writes words that have been written before
But in a different metre, with metaphors
And references that are not entirely theirs;
Poets have always had a way of persisting
Long after their lyres have lost their strings
And been put away in the cupboard;
Their voices have an only-too-familiar way
Of lingering, and of reminding us,
At unexpected times, of why it was

That we were initially so struck
By what they had to say to us:
Because we recognise it, because it is true.

You are certainly still there,
As real as the day before yesterday,
Saying all those familiar things
That seem every bit as important
As they were on that day when you
First said them, reminding us
To be human first of all, and then, if we can,
To delight, in our individual ways,
In the ordinary doings of folk
And the ways of nature, to look
With your eyes and your humour,
Your passions, too, at those around us;
To share your vision of what
It is that makes this normal life
So very precious, so amusing,
And so poignant – all of that.

We still need you, you know,
And you might be surprised
To hear just how deep and lasting
That need has turned out to be;
Especially now, when so much
Of what you wrote about
Seems a rather distant memory –
Fellowship in some inn somewhere,
A rural dance, time in the company

Of friends – things you put into song
That we think we remember
And that we'd like to experience again.

Of course, we can do that, with you
As our companion, Robert Burns,
The party is reconvened, the fellowship there
To be felt; the lights are on again.
Give us your hand – here's ours:
All Scotland, though a little quieter now,
Is a bit happier in your company,
A bit wiser in the light of what you wrote.

Every journey must end, and that may be at home – the most
glorious ending of all.

HOMECOMING

If there is one story that we, in our need for narrative,
Persistently ask for, it is a tale of homecoming;
The journey of a classical hero coming back from a war
To the uncertain reception of an importuned wife
Is one to which we have been listening
For an awfully long time; though we may know how it ends,
The beginning is still capable of fascinating
Even the most restless audience – difficulties
May abound, it seems, on even the most innocent
Journey back from the office; those who set off
On a route they have used time and time again
May still be surprised by the dangers that beset
The quotidian traveller; reaching home, it seems,
Is not always a forgone conclusion.

So we are always relieved when the haven we reach
Is revealed to be the right one, and waiting friends
Receive us with all the enthusiasm of those
Who have hoped for something that has now happened;
We may be accustomed to thinking of ourselves
As self-determining creatures, whose fate
Is firmly in hands we recognise as our own,
But the reality may be somewhat different:
If, when constructing an intricate machine,
The part we pick up clicks into place without argument,
If input and output match with a satisfying equivalence,
Then that may have nothing to with any design

We have elaborated ourselves; the cadence
That resolves a piece of music was probably there
Before Bach committed it to his populous staves;

But that need not worry us too much; what matters
Is that we finally reach our destination, the chapter
We're reading is ended, the book put away
And the light turned off; reaching home, we discover,
Is a process, long in the making, but not one
That those coming home ever mistake
For anything else; bands and ticker-tape
May be absent from the occasion of our return,
But we may be forgiven for imagining them,
And believing, even falsely, they are no less than our due:
Even the least of us, after all, may deserve to come home.